T0194980

LIVING
LIFE
Joyfully

JONI GUERNE

WESTBOW
PRESS®
A DIVISION OF THOMAS NELSON
& ZONDERVAN

WestBow Press books may be ordered through booksellers or by contacting:

WestBow Press
A Division of Thomas Nelson & Zondervan
1663 Liberty Drive
Bloomington, IN 47403
www.westbowpress.com
1 (866) 928-1240

Scripture quotations are taken from the Holy Bible, New Living Translation, copyright ©1996, 2004, 2015 by Tyndale House Foundation. Used by permission of Tyndale House Publishers, a Division of Tyndale House Ministries, Carol Stream, Illinois 60188. All rights reserved.

ISBN: 978-1-9736-9076-4 (sc)
ISBN: 978-1-9736-9078-8 (hc)
ISBN: 978-1-9736-9077-1 (e)

Library of Congress Control Number: 2020907561

Print information available on the last page.

WestBow Press rev. date: 05/27/2020

MANY THANKS

To my Proof Readers. They did an outstanding job.
This book is more enjoyable because of the work they did.
My heartfelt gratitude.

DEDICATION

This book is dedicated to my husband Mike.
My wonderful husband has been at my side every day,
He has been my constant aide and support.
Thank you Mike. For everything.

IN HONOR AND MEMORY

Of my mom
Shirley.
A wonderful wife, mom, grandmother, friend.

CONTENTS

FOREWORD

I thought it a bit odd that Joni asked me to write this. It is not that we don't go way back. We attended church together. Our kids played together. Our families took the kids to Sea World in a barely seaworthy RV. When I ran a Pain Management Support Group, she attended. I know how badly she has suffered. I often asked her, "What is wrong with you? Why are you always happy?" After reading her book, I now know the answer. Her joy was not so much about Joni, it was about Jesus.

Jim Van Treese, Ph.D
Licensed Psychologist

INTRODUCTION

Recently I was teaching a children's church lesson about Joy. The lesson plan was on the Fruits of the Spirit.

> But the Holy Spirit produces this kind of fruit in our lives: love, joy, peace, patience, kindness, goodness, faithfulness, gentleness, and self-control. There is no law against these things! (Galatians 5:22–23)

As I was teaching this lesson God was really speaking to me. He has been working with me for quite a while on the subject of 'joy', as I sometimes find it very difficult to live in joy, while at the same time living among the joy stealers. Living each day for me includes understanding and mastering the joy stealers of disease, pain, age, fatigue and others. Learning to navigate these challenges and the complications they often bring with them test my ability to listen to God and respond joyfully. These challenges can steal my joy if I do not keep my eyes on Jesus.

> I pray that God, the source of hope, will fill you completely with joy and peace because you trust in him. Then you will overflow with confident hope through the power of the Holy Spirit. (Romans 15:13)

God reminds me that we are not alone in this world of pain. My pain, your pain, any pain can steal joy. Physical pain, emotional pain, mental pain. It does not matter, the joy stealers are just waiting to jump in to take away our joy. But as we trust in God our source of hope He will fill us completely with both joy and peace that no joy stealer has a chance against.

I was diagnosed early in my twenties with a chronic illness. I was a wife and mother of 2 young children. Receiving the grim diagnoses was very discouraging. I was soon to learn though that God would be with me every step of the way, lifting me up, renewing my strength, and restoring my joy. When you have Jesus in your heart you never walk alone and you never face the joy stealers alone.

I wrote this book because I felt God wanted me to share with you, my readers, the clear and simple steps I have found effective at keeping the joy stealers away. Though we live in pain every day with God's help we can choose to say no to all the joy stealers and live in joy.

Examples of God active in people's lives and sending their joy stealers away and restoring their joy are used throughout the book. In Romans 15:13a we find a prayer that God will fill us completely with joy and peace because we trust in Him. I find as I read these examples in scripture where God restores someone's joy I begin to trust God more and more. And then as Romans 15:13b says I will overflow with confident hope through the power of the Holy Spirit! And when I overflow I can share my hope in Jesus with someone else.

> Therefore, go and make disciples of all the nations, baptizing them in the name of the Father and the Son and the Holy Spirit. Matthew 28:19

Because of God working in our lives, helping us in our weakness we are able to go and make disciples. The Holy Spirit gives us confident hope. Confident hope —enough for us and enough to go and tell others about Jesus.

> But those who trust in the LORD will find new strength. They will soar high on wings like eagles. They will run and not grow weary. They will walk and not faint. (Isaiah 40:31)

The scriptures remind us once again when morning comes and our bodies, minds, or emotions do not want to greet the day joyfully that when we trust in the Lord we find new strength. We will soar high over our problems and over the joy stealers like on wings of eagles. We will run and not grow weary and we will walk and not faint. And as we will find out in the coming pages we will run, yes we will run to our Lord and Savior Jesus Christ.

In His Name,
Joni Guerne

CHAPTER ONE

God changes my can'ts to cans

But I am trusting you, O LORD, saying, "You are my God!" My future is in your hands. (Psalm 31:14)

> The LORD is my strength and shield. I trust him with all
> my heart. He helps me, and my heart is filled with joy. I
> burst Out in songs of thanksgiving. (Psalms 28:7)

I am so glad that according to this scripture God is our strength because when I got out of bed this morning my strength was definitely not up to par. When I read this scripture and once again reminded myself that I did not have to rely on my own strength my joy returned and I was singing my praises to God. The joy stealers were there just waiting for me as I was attempting the challenge of getting out of bed, but they were soon sent packing as the God of our strength came and brought joy and strength. The joy stealers are constant companions on this journey of life, always working to steal my joy. But walking right beside me is the great joy giver, Jesus Christ. No joy stealer can stand against him.

One of the challenges I face is the attitude of, "I can't do it". This is a challenge I face daily. The joy stealers and I have an ongoing battle over the theory of whether the disease has control over my life or God does. I must always remind myself the disease is not who I am. Who I am is a child of the Most High God!

In my growing up years I was a baton twirler and I had a wonderful, terrific, instructor. One of her favorite sayings was, "Can't never could do anything." And she would not allow the word, "can't" in her studio. I try to remind myself of this as the joy stealers delight in reminding me of my limitations. God also knows my limitations, and blows right past them with this scripture.

> Do it with all the strength and energy that God supplies. Then everything you do will bring glory to God through Jesus Christ. All glory and power to Him forever and ever! (1Peter 4:11b)

I do not have to worry about "my" limitations because I serve and work with all the strength and energy that God gives me. I do not know what that scripture means to you, but to me it means everything! I do not rely on my strength and energy. Good thing, because I would not go very far relying on myself. God is my all in all. He is my energizer.

Fatigue is another issue that I deal with on a daily basis. There are many days that I find it very difficult to get up off the couch. I want to get up. I just cannot make myself due to deep fatigue. I am so thankful I have such a wonderful couch because there are times when I spend a lot of time on it! Fatigue is a very debilitating issue. It effects much more that your physical body. It effects your mental outlook and your emotional well-being. Dealing with fatigue is like walking through mud and fog at the same time. While dealing with fatigue, energy is in very short supply. Which makes it is very hard to fight against the joy stealers. It is very comforting to be reminded of this in God's Word.

> But those who trust in the LORD will find new strength. They will soar high on wings like eagles. They will run and not grow weary. They will walk and not faint. (Isaiah 40:31)

Take that joy stealers, I get my strength from my LORD, that is all I need. One of the most frustrating of the challenges is when flares happen and my physical body is unable to continue to meet the demands of my calendar. Which is a fancy way of saying when the challenges of disease, pain, and age, combine and make me unable to meet the demands of my everyday life, I become very frustrated. It saddens me to miss my grandson's ball games, or to miss Church activities. As I struggle with the concept of who is in charge of my schedule, the joy stealers are there just waiting for the opportunity to steal my joy. And then I am reminded of this scripture in Jeremiah.

> "For I know the plans I have for you," says the LORD.
> "They are plans for good and not for disaster, to give
> you a future and a hope." (Jeremiah 29:11)

God is teaching me again that joy comes as a free gift of the Holy Spirit, and because this joy comes from the Holy Spirit, it is Holy and set apart from earthly concerns. Joy is not dependent upon what is happening around us, and it is not swayed by others.

> Even though the fig trees have no blossoms, and there
> are no grapes on the vines; even though the olive crop
> fails, and the fields lie empty and barren; even though
> the flocks die in the fields, and the cattle barns are
> empty, yet I will rejoice in the LORD! I will be joyful in
> the God of my salvation! (Habakkuk 3:17-18)

Joy is a gift. When we accept this gift of the Holy Spirit and let the Holy Spirit guide and guard our joy, we will live a life full of joy and we will say:

> "With my whole being, body, and soul I will shout
> joyfully to the living God." (Psalm 84:2b)

> Our hearts ache, but we always have joy. We are poor,
> but we give spiritual riches to others, we own nothing,
> and yet we have everything. (2 Corinthians 6:10)

The Apostle Paul knows a lot about letting the Holy Spirit guard and guide his joy. In his 2nd letter to the Corinthian Church, Paul tells us that even though his mission team's heart ached they always had joy. What a wonderful testimony Paul gives to us in this letter. We often find it easy when we experience sorrow to let the joy stealers come in and steal our joy. But the Apostle Paul does not allow the joy stealers to steal his joy, and the next sentence in the verse may give us a clue as to why Paul remains joyful in all circumstances. "We are poor, but we give spiritual riches to others." (2 Corinthians 6:10a) No matter how poor in earthly riches Paul and his team are they share what they do have with others. And what they do have is faith, love and knowledge in the Lord and Savior Jesus Christ. If we listen carefully we can almost hear Paul joyfully proclaim, "We own nothing and yet we have everything!" (2 Corinthians 6:10b) I believe Paul's joy not only came from the Holy Spirit, but the Holy Spirit was the guide and guard of Paul's joy. It is with the Spirits help that we will be able to join with Paul and say, "Our hearts ache, but we always have joy." (2 Corinthians 6:10a) How is that? Remember, joy is not happiness. Happiness depends on life's circumstances. I am happy when the sun shines. I am happy when I get a day off work. I am joyful when I work, I am joyful when it is cloudy because joy is a gift of the Holy Spirit and the Holy Spirit will guard our joy! And yes, I am even joyful when I find myself spending the day on the couch. Sometimes it takes being reminded once again that joy is a gift before those joy stealers are sent away, but sent away they are! Am I still on the couch? Yes, I am. I am still on the couch, my situation has not changed, but the Holy Spirit is guarding my joy. And now my joy is filled and though my energy is low my joy is soaring high on wings like Eagles and I am singing praises to God.

As I read through the Bible, I am amazed at the truth that God wants us to live in joy. It is His desire that we live joyfully every day. In Paul's final instructions to the Christians in Thessalonica he wrote,

> Always be joyful. Never stop praying. Be thankful in all circumstances, for this is God's will for you who belong to Christ Jesus. (1 Thessalonians 5:16–18)

It is God's will for those who belong to Christ Jesus to always be joyful. This verse gives me both great comfort and confidence. As a Christian, when I asked Jesus to come and live in my heart, I chose to follow Jesus, to try and live my life in a way pleasing to Him. I find comfort that this verse tells us that it is God's will for us to be joyful, and I find confidence because I know that Jesus will not leave us hanging, alone, concerning something that is His will for our lives. If Jesus wills it, he will guide it, support it, and encourage it. The good news is that we do not have to do this joy thing all on our own because we have Jesus on our side. The same Jesus that healed the paralyzed man on the mat in Luke 5:18–20, and the man with leprosy in Mark 1:40–45a, loves us.

One thing I have learned is that God cares about us, about our whole selves, our physical, emotional, and spiritual, selves.

> "So don't worry about these things, saying, 'What will we eat? What will we drink? What will we wear?' These things dominate the thoughts of unbelievers, but your heavenly Father already knows all your needs. Seek the Kingdom of God above all else, and live righteously, and he will give you everything you need." (Matthew 6:31–33)

God knows what we need, of course he does, why does this surprise us, or why do we doubt this? We are much more valuable to God than the birds, yet look at the birds; they look carefree as they fly through the air. And they are not busy like the squirrels storing up food for the winter! The birds have figured out what we and our squirrel friends have not: God is El Shaddai – The God who supplies our needs. God who loves us and supplies all our needs, physical, emotional, and spiritual.

> When Abram was ninety-nine years old, the LORD appeared to him and said, "I am El Shaddai, 'God Almighty'. Serve me faithfully and live a blameless life. I will make a covenant with you by which I will guarantee to give you countless descendants." (Genesis 17:1–2)

God comes to Abram and introduces Himself as El Shaddai – The God who supplies all our needs. At that time Abram's greatest need was a son. God came and met that need. God, El Shaddai, God Almighty, the God who cares for us, met with Abram and made a promise to him. The God who cares for us will never break His promises. Paul tells us about El Shaddai in the Book of Acts. Paul is in the town of Lystra speaking to the people and says, "In the past he permitted all the nations to go their own ways, but he never left them without evidence of himself and his goodness. For instance, he sends you rain and good crops and gives you food and joyful hearts." (Acts 14:16–17). Here we find a wonderful example of our caring God always providing us with evidence of Himself. I wonder as I stand in awe of the sunrise, so beautiful, with hints of red this morning, who could look on such beauty and not come to worship the Living God, who made heaven and earth, the sea, and everything in them? God supplies our needs by providing food and joyful hearts. Yes, that is who El Shaddai is, the God who supplies our needs by providing not only evidence of himself and his goodness but also takes care of our physical needs. With El Shaddai providing our joy, the Holy Spirit guiding and guarding our Joy and Jesus on our side, the joy stealers will soon be sent away empty-handed.

THOUGHTS ON LIVING JOYFULLY:

Galatians 5:22 and 23a – But the Holy Spirit produces this kind of fruit in our lives: love, joy, peace, patience, kindness, goodness, faithfulness, gentleness, and self-control. The Author states that, "Joy is a gift of the Holy Spirit and is Holy and set apart from earthly concerns". How does this statement affirm or differ from your understanding of Joy?

How can you let the Holy Spirit guide and guard your joy and enable you to live a life so full of joy you will, "Sing praises to God, our strength." (Psalm 81:1).

> Our hearts ache, but we always have joy. We are poor, but we give spiritual riches to others. We own nothing, and yet we have everything. (2 Corinthians 6:10)

Take a moment and reflect on whether you have ever felt like Paul in this verse in 2 Corinthians.

1 Thessalonians 5:16 – On a daily basis how difficult is it for you to, "always be joyful"? What is keeping you from being joyful always?

Meditate on knowing if Jesus wills it, he will guide it, support it, and encourage it.

Two of the authors biggest joy stealers are pain and fatigue. Take a few minutes and contemplate what conditions or situations steal your joy.

"The birds have figured out what we and our squirrel friends have not: God is El Shaddai – The God who supplies all our needs." Are you more like a bird – care free and calm or more like a squirrel, busy, doing, and fretting?

How hard is it for you to fully rely on El Shaddai?

"For instance, he sends you rain and good crops and gives you food and joyful hearts." (Acts 14:17b) - What is one way today you can begin to rely on God and receive the joy He has for you?

When we are able to begin to fully rely on God we will be on the way to a joy filled Life.

CHAPTER TWO

I am my brother's keeper

*The young women will dance for joy and the men -old and young —
will join in the celebration. I will turn their mourning into joy. I will
comfort them and exchange their sorrow for rejoicing. (Jeremiah 31:13)*

Joy in the midst of one of the joy stealers. Tonight, Sunday night, the
one night of the week I really look forward to. Sunday evening I meet
with a group of Christians for bible study, fellowship, encouragement,
mutual support and prayer. This group has been together for many
years, through life's ups and downs, through much laughter and tears.
We very rarely cancel a bible study as we all value our time together,
understanding that if we miss a gathering, that may be the night one of
us really needs to share their burden and be encouraged and lifted up
by our group. As the scripture in Jeremiah says, "I will exchange their
sorrow for rejoicing". (Jeremiah 31:13b), a burden shared among a group
of caring, praying Christians can lift the burden and turn the burden
from sorrow to joy. With Jesus as our center and as our focus our burden
becomes lighter and when shared among Christian friends — sorrow
shared can become joy shared.

The believers devoted themselves to the apostles teaching, and to fellowship and to sharing in meals (including the Lord's Supper), and to prayer. (Acts 2:42)

Luke tells us, in these verses in Acts what was important to the early Church when they gathered together. In fact Luke says the believers devoted themselves to learning, fellowship, sharing in meals and prayer. They "devoted themselves" to meeting together in joint activities. When I think of the Sunday night Bible Study Group I belong to, I believe we not only value our time together, I would say we are devoted to it. Devoted and loyal in attendance each week. Devoted and loyal to prayer for one another. Devoted and loyal in caring for one another and building one another up, encouraging each other to better serve our Lord and Savior Jesus Christ. One of the things the early believers and my Sunday night Bible Study Group have in common is both have made fellowship a priority. It seems that fellowship has gotten a bad name lately, fellowship has come to equate with gossip. Not so. We need fellowship, the gathering of the believers. The writer of the New Testament Book of Hebrews understood this very well when he wrote,

"Let us think of ways to motivate one another to acts of love and good works. And let us not neglect our meeting together, as some people do, but encourage one another, especially now that the day of his return is drawing near. (Hebrews 10:24–25)

When one of the joy stealers come and we find our sorrow overcoming our joy, God uses our fellow believers to encourage us and build us back up and restore our joy. Sitting at home, facing our joy stealer it is oftentimes hard to keep our joy. It is when we are meeting together, that our Christian friends come next to us with Christian care and concern and lift us up to the true joy bringer, Jesus Christ. The One who heals our hearts and turns our mourning into joy.

Sometimes we lift up the one needing prayer, and sometimes the one needing prayer lifts us up. Part of our group is an awesome couple. They continue to lift us up with their presence. Laughter soon rings out whenever they are able to attend. You see, she is fighting cancer. Has been for many years. In fact she has won the battle against cancer for so long that it is hard for those of us who know and love this strong, tough, Christian woman to acknowledge that her time on earth is getting short. Or the train to heaven is slowing down for her. She has so often looked cancer in the eye and said not today. I have been on the receiving end of that look in her eye and the question, "well?" And I know I am about to have a change of direction in my life, like so many before me in her cross hairs. What an awesome woman. With an awesome husband at her side. With an ear for the Holy Spirit, and his love for her only more for his Lord. They bring so much joy and faith. They know our Lord, and that our lives here on earth are only temporary. And both of them are determined to do God's work for every minute they are here on earth. What joy! We thank God for putting them in our lives and pray He will keep joy in their hearts. May she continue to do God's work every day!

When we meet together in fellowship with other believers we have the opportunity to share with each other what is happening in our lives. In fellowship we have time to share with each other, share our joys and our burdens with each other, time to spend listening to each other, to learn from each other. Not just bumping up against each other with a quick, "Hi, how are you?" and then moving on without listening to the answer. During times of fellowship believers have the opportunity to learn the cares and concerns of their Christian friends, which not only makes prayer much more meaningful, but also gives our Christian friends the opportunity to understand how best to come beside us to help restore our joy.

> Some men came carrying a paralyzed man on a sleeping mat. They tried to take him inside to Jesus, but they couldn't reach him because of the crowd. So they went up to the roof and took off some tiles. Then they lowered the sick man on his mat down into the crowd, right in front of Jesus. Seeing their faith, Jesus said to the man, "Young man, your sins are forgiven." (Luke 5:18–20)

"Is it easier to say, 'Your sins are forgiven,' or 'Stand up
and walk'? So I will prove to you that the Son of Man
has the authority on earth to forgive sins." Then Jesus
turned to the paralyzed man and said, "Stand up, pick up
your mat and go home!" And immediately, as everyone
watched, the man jumped up, picked up his mat, and
went home praising God. (Luke 5:23–25)

In these verses in Luke we find the story of a paralyzed man with
friends who are determined to help restore his health and his joy. They
come carrying him, to lay him before Jesus – the true Healer and Joy
Giver. When they find they are unable to bring their paralyzed friend
into the house where Jesus is because of the crowd, they are not deterred.
They decide to take their friend up on the roof to lower him down after
cutting a hole in the roof tiles. I do not know about you, but I wish I
could have heard that conversation. You see, I have been the, 'man on
the mat'. And as the, 'man on the mat', the last thing I want to do is draw
attention to myself. I get more than enough attention just by being,
'on' the 'mat'. I really, really, do not want any more attention, thank you
very much. Now, placing myself here...in this situation...When my friend
came with the idea to bring me to the Great Healer – joy giver, it did
not take much convincing to get me to agree to load up on my mat for
the ride to see Jesus. But when we get to the house, oh no, the crowd!
And now these wonderful friends have this harebrained idea to drag me
up on the roof? And lower me through a hole they cut in the ceiling?
Nope. Not going to happen. I can already feel everyone staring at me.
I know people stare at me because I'm on this mat, oh, I do not want to
give people another reason to stare at me.

Two things to recognize here. First, one of the biggest joy stealers
is chronic illness. Illness of any kind steals our joy and makes us forget
that we are made in God's image. Not only is our body hurting from the
illness; our self-image, because of the effects of the illness is very low and
it is very difficult to find our joy. Chronic illness causes many different
and difficult changes to the body. Since my illness the fluctuations in my
weight alone have been difficult on my self-image (as I know they are on
many of my, 'Living with Pain' friends). Also, every time illness causes

me to miss a family or Church activity, my self-image and confidence takes a nose dive that is hard to recover from. The joy stealers are there telling me I was not good enough to go anyway. joy stealer– confidence breaker. With both my joy and confidence level low it is difficult to put myself in situations that draw more attention to me and my illness. I have learned that these situations often leave me less than my best and vulnerable to the joy stealers.

The Second thing to recognize is the determination of the friends in our scripture in the gospel of Luke. As determined as I might be to saying, "Ah, we will catch Jesus another day." The friends are even more determined that this is the day to meet Jesus. Again, seeing this situation through my eyes, I know my Christian friends will not accept any excuses from me, to keep me from meeting Jesus the great healer and joy giver. Just like the friends in the verses in the gospel of Luke, my Christian friends lift me up to bring me into the presence of Jesus.

In verse 25 after the paralytic receives his healing from Jesus he jumps up, picks up his mat and goes home, praising Jesus. I can feel the man's joy shine through this verse. I can almost see him dancing as he returns home filled with joy. I imagine his joy was so great to overflowing that it became joy shared.

> "The Young women will dance for joy and the men – old and young – will join in the celebration." (Jeremiah 31:13a)

> Don't copy the behavior and customs of this world, but let God transform you into a new person by changing the way you think. Then you will learn to know God's will for you, which is good and pleasing and perfect. (Romans 12:2)

Once we have met Jesus, after we have had a life changing experience with the Savior of the World, we become a child of the Most High God. We no longer are shackled by the sin that kept us from living a full joyful life. Just like the paralytic, in the story in the Gospel of Luke, who was bound by being unable to walk until he encountered Jesus. When he met Jesus face to face, Jesus set him free by healing him, which set him free from his physical limitations and Jesus set him free spiritually by forgiving him of his sins. The man, who could now jump and walk because he was healed physically, was saved and forgiven, and bursting with joy. After we are saved and forgiven we must act like it, speak like it, and be like it. Our very attitudes must be of saved, redeemed children of the Most High God. As long as we remember who we are in Christ we will be able to keep the joy stealers away, but once we begin thinking we are who we were before we were saved, we give the joy stealers the opening they need to come in and steal the joy we received when Jesus saved us from our sins. At the time Jesus saves us we become a new creation in Christ Jesus. A New you.

> "Let God transform you into a new person by changing
> the way you think." (Romans 12:2)

Our old way of life is such a big part of us that it is going to take God to transform us into the new person He wants us to be. This is more than likely not something we will be able to do on our own. But, the Good News is that Jesus has our back! If God wills it he will guide it, support it, and encourage it. We do not have to change how we think all on our own because we have Jesus on our side. When we accepted Jesus as our Savior we became a new creation in Christ Jesus, and God's Will for us is good and pleasing and perfect. And that is something to rejoice about.

I have heard some Christians refer to themselves as, "just poor sinners, saved by Grace." I believe that as soon as we continue to think of ourselves as, 'sinners', instead of, 'children of the Most High God, redeemed and transformed into a new creation', we are allowing the joy stealers to come in and steal the joy of our Salvation. By focusing on our continued status as a, 'sinner', we are first of all, forgetting all the joy we received when we heard Jesus whisper those words, 'You are forgiven'. And second, by hanging on to the label of, 'sinner', we also, however unintentionally are giving ourselves an excuse to continue sinning. I myself think Jesus calls us to set our eyes on our new creation in Christ Jesus. Jesus is the Life Changer and Joy Bringer. He will send those joy stealers running when we keep our eyes focused on our new life in Him and let Him do a new work in our lives.

THOUGHTS ON LIVING JOYFULLY:

> All the believers devoted themselves to the apostles
> teaching, and to fellowship, and to sharing in meals,
> (Including the Lord's Supper), and in prayer. (Acts 2:42)

The scripture in Acts tells us the early Church believed fellowship was a priority in their Christian walk. Looking at your times of fellowship with other believers would you say you were devoted and loyal to your fellowship group?

Do you have a fellowship group you can share your joys and burdens with? If not, spend some time contemplating where you can find a group to join or step out in faith and start one.

Luke 5:23–25 tells us of a paralyzed man being carried by some men as they tried to take him into see Jesus. Have you ever been the, "man on the mat"? If so, how did the experience change your understanding of joy?

How did the experience bring you closer to Jesus? Spend a moment considering how this man may have felt.

What is one of your biggest joy stealers? Spend some time considering what situations leave you vulnerable to the joy stealers.

The "friends", in this scripture are determined to bring the paralyzed man into the presence of Jesus. Consider the friends in your life that will accept no excuses from you, to keep you from meeting Jesus, the Great Healer and Joy Giver. Thank God in prayer for these faithful friends.

When the paralyzed man met Jesus, his sins were forgiven. God transformed him into a new person. Have you experienced this life changing joy filled moment when Jesus washed your sins away? If not you may want to pause and spend time in prayer to our Lord and Savior Jesus Christ, repenting of your sins and asking for his forgiveness. Ask Jesus to become Lord of your life and you will know peace and joy everlasting.

Romans Chapter 12 verse 2 tells us to "let God transform you into a new person by changing the way you think." We are called to set our eyes on our new creation in Christ Jesus. What is one way you can keep focused on your new life in Christ? Jesus is the Life Changer and Joy Bringer. When we allow God to change the way we think we will be on the way to a joy filled life.

CHAPTER THREE

Monkeys, chipmunks, and hippos! Oh my!

Satisfy us each morning with your unfailing love, so we may sing for joy to the end of our lives. (Psalm 90:14)

Mornings. Some people are morning people, some people are not. Either way, a fan of mornings or not, mornings come every day. At my house I usually set my alarm so I do not oversleep and am late getting to the pool for my daily exercise. Of course setting my alarm is unnecessary, because about an hour before the alarm is due to go off my cute little dog wakes me up. Every morning. Now on those nights where I have not gotten a lot of sleep, when she wakes me up before my alarm, I am a bit challenged to remember her cuteness. Not that she isn't just as cute on those days, but her cuteness has a difficult time penetrating through my fog of tiredness. Because of my lack of sleep I have missed out on the joy this little dog brings each morning. When I was a teenager my mother delighted in waking me up with the statement, "wake up, you do not have to sleep any more", (yes, as a teenager you can imagine how funny I thought that was!) This is what I believe is going through my little dog's brain: "Get up, get up, you do not have to lay in that bed sleeping any more, you can get up and play with me now." What joy! She cannot wait to meet the day with me. Now, I can begin my day embracing this joy or through a sleep deprived fog stumble through the morning totally missing the joy God has given me in this little dog who brings me outside each day to see the beauty of God's miracle of the sunrise. Oh Lord, thank you for each new day. How we greet this day is up to us. We can welcome and accept the joy God gives or we can miss His joy and continue with our lives wondering why our lives are dull and joy-less.

God sends His joy to us in many different ways. My mornings begin with the joy brought by my little dog, and continue with the joy of watching the beauty of God's sunrise. Once we open our eyes and our hearts to God's gift of joy we find that God is willing and able to fill us with joy to overflowing. I believe God is always willing to offer us His joy; it is us who can sometimes get in the way of receiving this wonderful gift of joy.

> "I have loved you even as the Father has loved me. Remain in my love. When you obey my commandments, you remain in my love, just as I obey my Father's commandments and remain in his love. I have told you these things so that you will be filled with my joy. Yes, your joy will overflow. This is my commandment: love each other in the same way I have loved you." (John 15:9–12)

I love these verses from the Gospel of John. Jesus is talking to his disciples, to his future disciples and to future believers. What comfort we receive to know our Savior loves us. Jesus loves us and wants to fill us with his joy, joy overflowing. How do we stay connected to Jesus, so our love connection remains strong? We love each other as Jesus has loved us. Oh sounds so simple, and yet is so hard to do. Show others the grace Jesus shows me. Give others the second, and third, and fourth, and eight hundredth chance that Jesus gives me. Be patient with others as Jesus is with me. Love others every day in every way, and never stop. That is what we are called to do. And yes, the joy we will know will overflow, and never end. What could be better than receiving Jesus's joy? Better than being filled with the joy of Jesus? So filled with the joy of Jesus that our joy is overflowing. I think that if we walked in this joy every day we would have enough joy to share with others, in fact we would just be bursting to share our joy. The joy of Jesus is joy unending, and a joy so strong that no joy stealer can stand against it.

> A man with leprosy came and knelt in front of Jesus, begging to be healed. "If you are willing, you can heal me and make me clean," he said. Moved with compassion, Jesus reached out and touched him. "I am willing," he said. "Be healed!" Instantly the leprosy disappeared, and the man was healed. Then Jesus sent him on his way with a stern warning: "Don't tell anyone about this. Instead, go to the priest and let him examine you. Take along the offering required in the Law of Moses for those who have been healed of leprosy. This will be a public testimony that you have been cleansed." But the man went and spread the word, proclaiming to everyone what had happened. (Mark 1:40-45a)

A man with Leprosy came to Jesus and "begged" for healing. Leprosy is a chronic infectious disease. As the disease progresses it can cause paralysis and disfigurement. Today this disease is treatable, whereas in New Testament times it was not. Leprosy at that time was something to be feared. Once a person was infected with leprosy they immediately had to withdraw from their family and community and move to live outside the city, either by themselves or in a leper community. As a person with leprosy they were now considered unclean and could have no contact with other people. People with leprosy could not be near other people or even speak to anyone. If the Leper came close to someone, they had to shout out, "unclean, unclean," to warn them that someone with leprosy was in the vicinity. As if being kicked out of their community and separated from their family was not awful enough, their self-esteem took a further hit by not only being denied contact with anyone, but also having to loudly declare their physical condition to everyone within hearing distance.

Lepers lived outside the city, often in caves, alone or in groups with other lepers. As no one else would have any contact with them, the lepers depended on themselves or other lepers for meeting their day-to-day needs. When we read in Mark 1:40 that "a man" with leprosy approached Jesus, I am somewhat surprised; where are the others in his leper community? I find it a little unusual that he is traveling alone. I wonder why he was the only one seeking the joy of Jesus's healing? Were the others in his leper community so overcome by the fog of being a leper outcast that they were missing out on this wonderful, awesome, life-changing, gift of joy? The joy stealers use many things to keep us from receiving the joy Jesus has for us. Our attitude of "I cannot do that," is one of the joy stealers methods. The other lepers may not have come to Jesus for fear of rejection. The people living with this disease have lived through many rejections and the idea of one more rejection may have been more than they could endure. This is another of the joy stealers methods. The joy stealers love to steal our joy before we receive it. When we feel the fog of this feeling overtaking us, we can take comfort and stand against the joy stealers from this verse in Philippians.

> "For I can do everything through Christ, who gives me strength." (Philippians 4:13.)

We can stand against the joy stealers because Christ gives us strength to stand against them. Christ, who wants our lives to be full of joy, gives us the strength to stand against the joy stealers. I think Philippians 4:13 is a verse that many of us need to write down and put up in key locations around our homes. This verse is that important. I need to be reminded of this often during the day. Yes, I <u>can</u> do everything through Christ. Yes, <u>Christ</u> gives me <u>strength.</u> (Underline added by author) At every attack of the joy stealers we can firmly send them running, knowing Christ stands with us. Jesus loves us so much that He went willingly to the Cross to forgive us and save us from our sins, so that our lives would be full of joy. Now that is reason to rejoice, and wake up every morning with joy in our hearts. It does not matter to Jesus what you look like, what you have done, or how tired you are; Jesus loves you and wants to fill your life with joy.

Jesus took on his body our sins, went to the cross, and his body showed the price he paid for you and me. There are not any joy stealers I know of that are strong enough to stand against this great joy giver, that loved us so much that he endured, not only death on the cross, but also being pierced and crushed and beaten and whipped. He paid the price, and by his wounds redeemed us and healed us. The next time you are running short on your joy meter and you feel the joy stealers coming near remember Isaiah 53:5, "But he was pierced for our rebellion, crushed for our sins. He was beaten so we could be whole. He was whipped so we could be healed." Jesus stood in the gap so we could live a joy-filled life. Now that is reason to rejoice and wake up every morning. Jesus loves you and wants to fill your life with joy. Take that joy stealers! It does not matter to Jesus what you look like, what you have done or how tired you are.

> "Don't tell anyone about this. Instead, go to the priest and let him examine you. Take along the offering required in the Law of Moses for those who have been healed of leprosy. This will be a public testimony that you have been cleansed. But the man went and spread the word, proclaiming to everyone what had happened."
> (Mark 1:40–45a)

Jesus instructs the man who has been healed not to tell anyone about what has happened, to just go give the required offering. Jesus wants to keep this as low key as possible, to keep the news from spreading. But the man finds this impossible to do. I think he was so full of joy to overflowing it did just that – over flowed! In verse 41 we read that Jesus, moved with compassion, reached out and touched him. I wonder when the last time this man, this leper was touched with hands of love and compassion. And then in verse 42 we find him healed of the leprosy by Jesus. No low key here! I think this man is dancing for joy! Have you ever had such good news you just could not keep it to yourself? News of a birth of a baby? An engagement of your child? Upcoming retirement? Joyful occasions where you just cannot keep the news in.

A few years back a set of first time Grandparents at my home church just found out the wonderful news. A time of rejoicing, right? Well, of course the joy stealers use every opportunity to steal our joy. A disagreement, a disappointment over which set of Grandparents was to announce the, "Good News" to the Church, and soon there was no rejoicing. The joy stealer came and stole the joy both sets of Grandparents should have had. As the Grandparents were arguing about which one was to have the honor of the announcement the joy stealer traded bitterness and misery for the joy that Jesus offered them. The man healed of leprosy understood the joy of the Lord. He 'proclaimed' what had happened. He told what Jesus did. He gave Glory to God. The two new sets of Grandparents to be, only had eyes for themselves, which made it easy for the joy stealers. When we keep our focus on Jesus, on His Glory, on His strength, we keep the joy stealers out and we are soon dancing with joy. We have so much joy; we like the man with Leprosy, have to share it. I think that is how Jesus wants us to live all the time.

"Satisfy us each morning with your unfailing love, so we may sing for joy to the end of our lives." (Psalm 90:14)

Wow. Sing for joy, not for a day, or a week or a year, but until the end of our lives. That is a lot of joy. Every Day! Joy for today. When we wake up, each morning remember God loves you, and reach for your joy. God is ready to give it to you. Where is it? Most mornings when I look in the mirror it is, Yikes! As my hair is beyond control. I either find joy in the mirror or look for the scissors! (I find joy that the dog woke me up early so I can fix this hair before I scare someone beside myself!) Where do you find joy? Sometimes we have to look behind the clouds the joy stealers are putting up. God has joy for you. The God who made the zebra and the hippo and the monkey is in the joy business. Who cannot smile when thinking of zebras, hippos and monkeys? And while you are smiling take time to share that smile with someone. It might bring them some joy and help them turn away the joy stealers.

> The faithful love of the Lord never ends! His mercies never cease. Great is his faithfulness; his mercies begin afresh each morning. I say to myself, "The LORD is my inheritance; therefore, I will hope in him!" (Lamentations 3:22–24)

I find early in the morning when we are just beginning to face the day, the joy stealers are way more active than we are. This is a time when we really need to be aware that the joy stealers are present and just waiting to steal the joy God has for us. But God is faithful; God is there ahead of us and before the joy stealers. Our hope is in Him. The joy stealers cannot stand against him.

> The faithful love of the Lord never ends! His mercies never cease. Great is his faithfulness; (Lamentations 3:22–23)

God's mercies begin afresh each morning. When we wake up, God's mercies – his blessings, his new mercies and blessings are waiting for us. That is an awesome thought, that God loves us so much that yesterday is over and today is a new day with new blessings and new joys. What are we going to do with this wonderful new day God has given us? He has given us a new day and given us a starter boost by adding his blessing to the beginning of the day. We are ahead of the game before we ever get out of bed! What joy we have!

THOUGHTS ON LIVING JOYFULLY:

Psalm 90:14 tells us the Psalmist asks for the Lord to, "Satisfy us each morning with your unfailing love." As God is willing and able to fill us with joy over flowing, what are some of the ways you sometimes get in the way of receiving His wonderful gift of joy?

John 15:9-12 tells us Jesus loves us and wants us to remain in His love. According to this verse in order to remain in His love we are to obey His commandment and love each other in the same way He has loved us. What do you find the most difficult about loving others every day, in every way, and never stopping?

The joy we will know will overflow and never end. Spend some time thinking about having so much joy it over flows in all you do and say.

Mark 1:40-45 tells about a man with Leprosy that comes to Jesus and begs to be healed. Have you ever been separated from your family because of an illness or disease? How did the separation affect you? If not, take a moment and consider what it would be like to be separated from your family and community and denied contact with anyone because of a disease you had.

The joy stealers use many things to keep us from receiving the joy Jesus has for us. What are some of the attitudes or methods that the joy stealers use to keep you from receiving the joy Jesus has for you. What is the most effective attack method of the joy stealers?

Philippians 4:13 – Since Jesus gives us the strength to stand against everything that tries to steal our joy, do you use His strength to stand strong against everything that comes against you? Why or why not?

Isaiah 53:5 – How do you feel knowing Jesus took the punishment on his body for our sins?

Jesus instructs the man with Leprosy, who has been healed, not to tell anyone about what has happened. But the man finds this impossible to do. Think of a time that you were so filled with joy that the joy just overflowed. Then take a few moments and praise God for joy overflowing.

When Jesus touched the man with Leprosy it may have been the 1st time in a long time that the man was touched at all. How important is human touch to you? Spend a moment to consider spending a week without experiencing any human contact. What do you believe the effect on you would be?

Psalm 90:14 Satisfy us each morning with your unfailing love, so we may sing for joy to the end of our lives. When we wake up each day God is ready to fill our lives with joy – whether we are ready to receive the joy or not. Some of us are morning people, some are not. Either way, remember each morning God loves you and reach for your joy. God is ready and willing to give it to you.

Consider what hinders you from receiving the joy God has for you each morning. Not joy just for a day – but joy so you may sing to the end of your life. Imagine singing for joy to the end of your life, praising God for his blessings. Lamentations 3:22-24 When we wake-up, God's blessings are waiting for us. What are you going to do with this wonderful new day God has given you?

When we begin to realize God has given us a starter boost to the day, by adding His blessing to the beginning, we will be on the way to a joy filled life.

CHAPTER FOUR

Take two steps and call on Jesus

One day Jesus said to his disciples, "Let's cross to the other side of the lake." So they got into a boat and started out. As they sailed across, Jesus settled down for a nap. But soon a fierce storm came down on the lake. The boat was filling with water, and they were in real danger. The disciples went and woke him up, shouting, "Master, Master, we're going to drown!" When Jesus woke up, he rebuked the wind and the raging waves. Suddenly the storm stopped and all was calm. Then he asked them, "Where is your faith?" The disciples were terrified and amazed, "Who is this man?" they asked each other. "When he gives a command, even the wind and waves obey him." (Luke 8:22–25)

In these verses in the Gospel of Luke, Jesus and his disciples are in a boat crossing the Sea of Galilee when a sudden storm comes up. It was not unusual for storms of this kind to appear unexpectedly on this body of water. When the storm arrives the disciples, some who are experienced fisherman, are frightened. I am thinking this must have been quite a ferocious storm to scare these disciples. Now, me, I am not a boat person.

At the first big wave I am calling on Jesus! These verses tell us we will find Jesus asleep, taking a nap. The Gospel of Mark 4:35-41 tells us Jesus was asleep in the, "back" of the boat. (Now, not being a boat person, I have no idea what you call the "back" of the boat), and the disciples, like me, turn to him and shout, "we are going to drown." Jesus woke up and took quick action calming the storm. The storm outside and the storm inside the disciples. The joy stealers had come while Jesus was sleeping and in just a few moments they had stolen all the disciple's joy. For I believe this storm raged on the Sea of Galilee while at the same time it raged inside the frightened disciples. Verse 24 says, "We are going to drown!" The joy stealers had done such a good job, they had made the disciples not only doubt themselves and their ability to handle the boat, but also forget who Jesus was.

In verse 25 Jesus asks the disciples, "Where is your faith?" I think Jesus is asking, "Where is your trust in me?" The disciples were frightened and confused, unfamiliar feelings for these rugged men of Galilee. Jesus ever so gently reminded them of who they were and whose they were. They were Jesus's disciples and by their faith in him they belonged to Jesus's family. When the joy stealers come and bring the storms that swamp your "boat", to the point that you begin doubting yourselves, the same way the disciples did, hold on to Jesus. He is there for you. He is there to calm your storms. Some of the disciples were very experienced fishermen, experienced in fishing in this very sea. Yet the joy stealers brought so much confusion and doubt that they forgot who they were. The first thing they did was call out to Jesus, and when we experience the coming of the joy stealers that is our first response also.

When we face the storms of our lives we need the one who calms the storms. I know that at the first big wave, when I shout out, "Jesus, help me!" Jesus will take quick action to calm my storm. When the waves threaten to swamp us we can know that we are not in the "boat" alone. Jesus is in the "boat" with us and he has our back. We can face the storms of life because we have the one who calms the storms with us. We can withstand the storm and the joy stealers because we never stand alone.

> The Lord is my strength and shield. I trust him with all
> my heart. He helps me, and my heart is filled with joy. I
> burst out in songs of thanksgiving. (Psalm 28:7)

The Lord is our strength and shield. We hold on to Him when the
joy stealers come. His shield covers us. His shield gives us the ability
to resist the joy stealers and will protect us from future sneak attacks
from them. For joy stealers love to come when our guard is down, but
the wonderful, amazing good news is that God's guard, God's shield is
never down! His shield is always covering us. He helps us and we are
filled with joy! We are, yes, we are! And we sing out in Thanksgiving.
For God – El Shaddai – The God who supplies all our needs and cares
for us will never leave us or forsake us. We trust in Him. El Shaddai – All
Mighty God – Our Strength and Our Shield.

> Just then a woman who had suffered for twelve years with
> constant bleeding came up behind him. She touched the
> fringe of his robe, for she thought, "If I can just touch his
> robe, I will be healed." Jesus turned around, and when he
> saw her, he said, "Daughter, be encouraged! Your faith
> has made you well." And the woman was healed at that
> moment. (Matthew 9:20–22)

I wonder if when this poor woman woke up that morning she realized
that God's mercies never cease and that they are new every morning.
I wonder if God blessed her with fresh joy by telling her that this was
the day she would meet Jesus. Did she know she was ahead of the game
before she ever got out of bed?

In Matthew 9:20 we find that this woman had a constant bleeding
for 12 years. Now that is a very long time. For 12 years she had suffered
through the social disgrace of the "issue of blood". By Jewish law and
regulation a woman with an issue of blood was considered 'unclean'. By
being declared unclean a person was identified as morally and spiritually
defiled and could have no physical contact with anyone, or that person
would become unclean. No physical contact with anyone. She could
not touch or be touched, for 12 years. Also, according to Leviticus

15:26, any bed or any chair a woman sat on was considered unclean and no one could touch it or they also would become unclean. As a result of these restrictions women often withdrew in seclusion. Did the joy stealers come and bring 12 years of seclusion to this woman, 12 years of loneliness?

I cannot imagine the isolation and loneliness I would feel after being forced from my home and family for 12 years. Loneliness is one of the joy stealers that is very hard to stand against. Loneliness is one of the sneaky joy stealers that comes in so quietly that it gets a foothold before we even know it has come and stolen our joy. Unfortunately, loneliness does not usually travel alone. It has another joy stealer as a travel companion, and her name is depression. These two joy stealers love sneak attacks. I believe this woman, after being unable to hug her family for 12 years would at the least be fighting against these two joy stealers.

Family in the Jewish social tradition was very important. Unlike most people today, the Jewish people lived in large family units, sharing responsibility for chores and other obligations. The women in the Jewish family unit worked together to prepare and cook the food for the large family unit. As I am sure you have heard the old saying, "too many cooks spoil the soup", (or something like that!) I bet that made for some very interesting meal preparation. I know in my family, when we would get together for a large gathering at holiday time, preparation in the kitchen would be very entertaining as everyone had their own idea on how things should be done. Of course Grandma usually got her way no matter what advice was offered. For a Jewish woman in the family unit, besides working to prepare the meals, she also looked after the children. Taking care of the children was one of her prime duties. Caring for and educating both girls and boys for their first few years, and continuing to educate the girls in their duties of keeping the home. At that time the responsibility of teaching the boys was given over to their fathers.

A Jewish woman was very involved in the life of her family, from the moment she woke up, with meal preparation and continuing throughout the day with childcare and education. This family time involved interaction with other women and with the children in the family unit. Both of which in my experience are often fond of conversation. (I know this because all her life my granddaughter has loved to talk) The woman who had been bleeding for 12 years and had been excluded from her family unit must have missed these family interactions. After having no physical contact with her family and perhaps missing these social outlets, the loneliness must have become painful. I wonder if she had begun to forget who she was. Was she like the disciples in the boat during the storm on the Sea of Galilee? Did the joy stealers also bring doubt and confusion to her so she had begun to forget who she was?

Loneliness seems to never come to us alone. Loneliness brings along other feelings. When we suffer from loneliness we begin to feel that we deserve to be alone. That we are unworthy of having friends. Unworthy of having a family. Oh, the joy stealers are so good at what they do! Even in a crowded room our loneliness remains because the joy stealers have convinced us that we are unworthy of talking to anyone. That no one would possibly want to talk to us. Loneliness convinces us that we should stay home. That we are tired and we need to sleep. The joy stealers love it when we sleep all day, because when we sleep all day we are not serving God and furthering His Kingdom. Loneliness makes us short-tempered; because the joy stealers have convinced us to push others away, due to thinking that we are not worthy to have anyone in our life.

These are just some of the feelings that tag along with loneliness. The joy stealers love it when they steal our joy and stay around to keep our joy from coming back. We need to kick those joy stealers out, even though it will be hard when loneliness has set in.

> You thrill me, LORD, with all you have done for me! I
> sing for joy because of what you have done. (Psalm 92:4)

The first defense against the joy stealers is to remember what the Lord has done for you. Even if it is one thing. One blessing. I sing for joy because of what the Lord has done for me. I can think of no better starting spot. And the joy stealers really do not like this; they do not like us praising the Lord. Praise the Lord. Some days, when the joy stealers have paid me a visit, I begin by praising the Lord for the morning. I praise the Lord that I got out of bed that morning and that God gave me a new day, a new blessing. Thank you God for what you have done for me! Praising the Lord is the first step to getting rid of the joy stealers and keeping them away.

The Second step is to remember a joy blessing, for me it is my family. Nothing brings me more joy than my family. On the days when the joy stealers are near I have been known to call my daughter to see if my grandchildren can come visit. Because I know that when they walk through the door the joy stealers are sent running. The second step, remember a joy blessing, something that brings you instant joy. Remember your joy blessing and do not forget it! I hear my grandchildren coming and my heart rejoices, take that joy stealers! The other day was a rather frustrating day for me. I did not feel well, my body was hurting and telling me about it, and other things in my day had not gone well. When I heard my door open and two of my granddaughters came in talking and laughing. It was not long before one of my grandsons came in behind them. Oh, how my heart soared and my yucky day was quickly forgotten. My grandson and one of my granddaughters went outside to the basketball court, (that is, the driveway), the other granddaughter stayed inside and entertained me for an hour. Oh, I laughed and laughed. I do think she has a future in the theater! But, my point is, they came and lifted me up, and I soon forgot my aches and pains, and all the things that had gone wrong that day. Were all the aches and pains still there? Sure, I still hurt. But my blessings were shining through anything the joy stealers could throw at me. And later when I was having a bad time I would remember this blessing and I would defeat the joy stealers once again.

The third step against the joy stealers is your favorite scripture, or any scripture. I am sure you have noticed I have used a lot of scripture in this book, and that is because God's Word is a Mighty Defense against the joy stealers. When people ask me what my favorite scripture is it may change from day to day, as there are so many to choose from! Though my all-time favorite is:

> But those who trust in the LORD will find new strength.
> They will soar high on wings like eagles. They will
> run and not grow weary. They will walk and not faint.
> (Isaiah 40:31)

I quote this verse to the joy stealers whenever they try to tell me that fatigue will be my constant companion (another joy stealer). As I quote this verse I am reminded of Gods promise and the joy stealers are sent running. Find your scripture and remind the joy stealers of it, and repeat it and see the joy stealers start RUNNING!

THE fourth step in our defense against the joy stealers is our Christian friends. This is a difficult step when we are in the grip of loneliness. Step out in faith to a Christian friend and ask for a fellowship time. Christians do laugh. I know this is an unknown concept! When I get together with my Christian friends there is much laughter amid the talking (and the food, of course). I have a wonderful group of Christian friends who I fellowship with regularly. By sharing and laughing with these friends I am able to send the joy stealers running. Join a fellowship group or be bold and start one. Christian fellowship is very important to stand against the joy stealers. When we fellowship together the joy stealers are sent running.

The fifth step in our joy defense brings us back to our lonely Jewish woman who had been bleeding for 12 years. She was lonely, yes. A social outcast, yes. Still, she heard that Jesus was passing by, and like the disciples who turned to Jesus when the storm came, she thought, "If I can just touch his robe, I will be healed." (Matthew 9:21.)

Our fifth step is to turn to Jesus. He is our Strength and our Shield. This Jewish woman turned to Jesus and was healed and Jesus sent her joy stealers running,

> You have not done this before. Ask, using my name and you
> will receive, and you will have abundant joy. (John 16:24)

When we turn to Jesus, and ask, in His name, we will receive and we will have abundant joy. Large quantities of joy. Sounds like Jesus will send those joy stealers running!

These are just a few of the steps to send those joy stealers running: remember what the Lord has done, remember to find your joy blessing, repeat God's Word, Christian fellowship, and turn to Jesus. As we do these things we will become more and more comfortable with these steps. Some of the steps we may find easy to do, others may be uncomfortable, but the more we put these things into practice and experience the results, the easier the steps will become. The joy stealers will not be so quick to attack because they know that we are well prepared to defend against them. Perhaps most important the joy stealers know that Jesus has our back and that is reason enough to send them running!

THOUGHTS ON LIVING JOYFULLY:

Luke 8:22–25 – When life's storms come and the joy stealers are trying to steal your joy do you reach out for Jesus or try to steer through the storm on your own?

Psalm 28:7 – The Psalmist declares, "I trust him with all my heart". Spend some time contemplating your, "trust level", and how it may be possible to trust God with all your heart.

Matthew 9:20–22 – In the Jewish culture family was very important. Considering the woman, who had suffered for twelve years with constant bleeding, it is possible the joy stealers used her illness, which separated her from her family, to bring her, depression, doubt, and confusion, among other emotions. What emotions do you sometimes find it difficult to deal with?

The joy stealers are so good at what they do! We need to kick those joy stealers out.

Psalm 92:4 Spend time today remembering what the Lord has done for you. The 1st defense against the joy stealers is praising the Lord. What will you praise the Lord for today?

The 2nd step in the defense against the joy Stealers is to remember a joy blessing, something that brings you instant joy. Remember your joy blessing and do not forget it. What is your joy blessing?

The 3rd step against the joy stealers is to recite or read your favorite scripture. God's Word is a mighty Weapon against the joy stealers. Spend some time in God's Word, considering what your favorite scripture is.

The 4th step against the Joy Stealers is to spend time in fellowship with other Christian believers. Consider how easy or difficult it is to fellowship with other believers. If you are able to fellowship with other believers, contemplate on your feelings after your time spent with other believers in fellowship and how you feel this will send the Joy Stealers away.

The 5th step against the Joy Stealers is to turn to Jesus. Reach out to Jesus. What are some ways you can turn to Jesus today?

John 16:24 – Ask, using Jesus's name and we will receive and have abundant Joy. Joy overflowing. Thank God today for giving you abundant Joy.

CHAPTER FIVE

With Jesus you've got this

But those who trust in the LORD will find new strength; they will soar high on wings like eagles. They will run and not grow weary. They will walk and not faint. (Isaiah 40:31)

For someone like myself who is fighting a chronic illness, this verse brings great joy. Strength is something that is very often in short supply in my life. Strength and energy are very quickly depleted, and it is a balancing act some days determining which activities I will be able to accomplish before fatigue takes over and I have no energy or strength left for the rest of the day. So when I read this verse: Those who trust in the LORD will find new strength. I cannot help but praise the Lord and thank Him for the strength he gives for each new day. This verse speaks to me especially on those days when the fatigue is so great that I do not have strength to put one foot in front of the other. I think if I just keep saying, "come on, feet, move it," this will help, but, nope, no go. These feet are not moving! When I try to do things in my own strength I fall flat on my face, (must be because these feet do not want to move), then I remember:

"Those who trust in the LORD will find new strength."

Yes, LORD, I trust in you. My trust is in you and in your Grace. I long for your New Strength, my old strength has run out and was never as good as this gift of New Strength given to those who trust in the LORD.

The beautiful news about this verse is that the Lord not only gives us strength, but gives us New Strength. In dealing with Chronic Illness we often times want our lives to go back to how they were before, before we were diagnosed, before the sickness came, before everything changed, before our friends left, before we were not in financial distress, before our spouse left, before... This verse tells us the Lord gives us strength – not the strength we had before, or the strength we have now, but a new strength. A strength, new, different – more powerful, more lasting. A strength that will soar high on eagles wings and run and not grow weary. When we soar on wings like Eagles we rise high above our problems and leave them in God's hands. When we leave our problems in God's hands our Joy is complete and the Joy Stealers are unable to steal our joy. When we try to handle our problems on our own instead of soaring on Eagles wings we are left on the ground and stuck in the mud. What do we find in the mud? Mud is thick and hard to move in and hard to get off once it gets on you. In the mud we find gossip and loneliness, darkness and joylessness because when we are stuck in the mud it is easy for the Joy Stealers to come in and steal every bit of our joy.

God made each of as individuals, different and unique. Each of us has their own God given gifts and talents. The other morning I was at the pool, doing my morning exercise. While I was in the water I got into a conversation with my husband and a dear friend of ours. (This was after I finished my exercise, really!) During the conversation one of them commented that they wished they could float, the other said they could float really well but wished they could sink. We often do not find joy in our abilities and gifts. The grass always seems greener on the other side of the fence. We need to rest in how God has made us and not let the joy stealers in to steal our joy in how God made us. God made us, loves us and will take care of us. Our joy comes from God and sends those joy stealers sinking to the bottom of the pool!

Recently I had a series of events that reminded me that life often gives us a basket full of lemons. Not one lemon, mind you, but a whole basket full. This is the time when everything around you appears to be falling apart. I say appears because we are only living in this very moment and do not see the full import of what God is doing in our lives. As each event occurred in my life and the lemons kept accumulating I began to feel like I was in a storm. A lemon storm. Lemons everywhere. Baskets full. I was reminded of the saying, "When life gives you lemons make lemonade." I thought about that saying, and decided if I did that I would still have lemons, they would just be mixed with water and sugar! Of course that is not a bad thing, turning something bitter into something sweeter. Turning the bitter events that had intruded into my life into sweeter happenings. As I was considering these things I remembered a Sunday school lesson I taught some time ago. Many youth in my class were becoming athletes and we were discussing the various ways they trained and the aids they used to get ready for their team. We also need to train for God's team. During that class we talked about how important it is to read our Bible every day. That is a priority in training for God's team. Daily prayer is another part of the training routine. We covered several parts of a Christian's daily walk, as they are a part of God's team. Being part of a team has some responsibilities and actions. Just like the athletes have aids to help them in their training so do we on God's team. As I taught the class that day I told them the Bible was the #1 aid we have to help us in our training, and to remember Jesus is always by our side. He will never leave us or forsake us.

> Anyone who believes in me may come and drink! For the scriptures declare, "Rivers of living water will flow from His Heart." (John 7:38)

A lemon storm is one of the joy stealers, while we are in the middle of the storm it is very hard to hang on to our joy. That is one reason it is so important to keep to our "training routine", so that when the storm comes and all we can see is lemons falling everywhere our "training" will kick in and our joy will bubble to the surface. Our joy will see those baskets of lemons and laugh and respond by saying I have Jesus, lemons do not affect my joy. God is by my side.

As I was in the middle of the storm, (the Lemon Storm), trying to keep to my training, I was in my normal spot on the couch wearing my very comfortable well-worn cozy sweats. Also known as sweat pants or jogging pants, though at the moment there was no sweating or exercising going on while wearing those pants. Those pants screamed I am having a super very bad yucky day, (svbyd). Yes that is right, svbyd. (super very bad yucky day). Take that to the mirror and look and see what is looking back at you. That my friend is a joy stealer. A big scary joy stealer, because we all have those days. Sometimes more than one at a time. How can we overcome this big and bad joy stealer? One way I work to send this joy stealer running is I change my earrings. For my birthday my family bought me some sparkly earrings. (I love sparkles!) I feel better just putting them on. Even though recently I was told there was an age limit for wearing sparkles. Hmm, who would have thought that? I decided I so blew past that age and have come around the corner, that I have reached the age where it is acceptable again! I look at that joy stealer and I fix my hair, and maybe put some make up on. Take that joy stealer! Now, it may take me several attempts to do these things, but I keep at it. Because even though I am wearing my svbyd sweats, it is important that I look like I feel terrific. I am a child of the Most High God. And I will present myself to Him in a worthy way. We honor God when we show Him our bodies are His temple. Believe me those joy stealers will take off running when they see us honoring God with our bodies. We may still be on the couch. We may still be stuck in the middle of a svbyd, but we will know that God is with us, beside us and guiding our way.

> Don't you realize that your body is the temple of the Holy Spirit, who lives in you and was given to you by God? You do not belong to yourself, for God bought you with a high price. So you must honor God with your body. (I Corinthians 6:19–20)

Then David gave Solomon the plans for the Temple and its surroundings, including the entry room, the storerooms, the upstairs rooms, the inner rooms, and the inner sanctuary—which was the place of atonement. (1 Chronicles 28:11)

"Every part of this plan," David told Solomon, "was given to me in writing from the hand of the LORD." Then David continued, "Be strong and courageous, and do the work. Do not be afraid or discouraged for the LORD God my God is with you. He will not fail you or forsake you. He will see to it that all the work related to the Temple of the LORD is finished correctly." (Chronicles 28:19–20)

This must be a magnificent Temple because our God is greater than all other gods. (2 Chronicles 2:5)

The writers of the Old Testament books of 1 Kings, 1 Chronicles and 2 Chronicles tell us of the beauty and magnificent of the temple of the LORD that Solomon built. The scripture in 1 Chronicles 28:19 tells us God gave David the instructions for building the temple. Every part and parcel of the temple was God ordained. The part of the Temple sectioned off for the Most Holy Place, (or inner Sanctuary) was the most beautiful. For the Most Holy Place was where God resided. When we read through the scriptures describing the materials used in the building of the temple with the understanding that each piece was ordained and designed by God it is awe inspiring. And then to remember that according to 1 Corinthians 6:19 -20 we are God's Temple. We are that beautiful, magnificent, God-designed Temple. Each of us has a Most Holy Place. God is waiting to come in and reside inside; all you have to do is ask Him to come into your life. When you do, you will never be the same.

When we ask Jesus into our lives we start to see the world through Jesus' eyes. As we see through the eyes of Christ our problems grow smaller and we grow closer to Jesus. Our problems grow smaller and our joy increases and the joy stealers have no place in our lives. The more we focus on God the bigger God becomes in our lives and the more insignificant our pain, problem, or situation becomes. When we focus on the pain, problem, or situation (pp&s) we give the pp&s more importance, and the, "bigger" it becomes and more important it becomes, and of course, then the more attention we pay to the pp&s. The more attention we pay to the pp&s the less attention we put on God. So the pp&s begin to block our access to God which then gives the joy stealers plenty of opportunity to come in and steal our joy because we have essentially blocked the main defense against the joy stealers out of our lives.

Whereas if we take the pp&s and say, we are "<u>NOT</u>" going to focus on you. Yes, we recognize you. But we are going to focus on God. The Life Changer. The One who gives us New Strength and lifts us up to Soar on Eagles Wings. The more we focus on God the bigger God becomes and our pp&s becomes smaller and more insignificant. When the joy stealers see how big God is in our lives it sends the joy stealers running.

One morning, (well, actually another morning), when I was at the pool for my daily exercise I had a rather significant pp&s. I go to the pool 5 days a week, when possible. I swim laps for exercise and also for stress relief, (believe me my family has been known to say, "Did you miss your swim today?") and for the wonderful time I spend with God praying, praising, and listening. My time in the pool is a joyful time – just me and God. What could be better? I have a very nice waterproof mp3 player, and I listen to Christian Music while I swim. Swimming, singing, praising, praying. What a joyful way to start the day! I wear a cross necklace, have for years. Add mp3 player, my swimming goggles, ear buds for my mp3 player and getting ready to get in the pool sometimes takes a while. So, this other morning I was swimming my laps, listening to my music, conversing with God, and all of a sudden I found I was slowly being strangled. The chain from my necklace became tangled with the cord from the ear buds for the mp3 player, and as my airway was being cut off, I thought, Uh oh, I need air! While swimming oxygen is very necessary, or you very quickly think you are going to drown. That was a moment I could have let the joy stealers in to steal all the joy from my morning of swimming, or I could choose joy. I had been focusing on God and on how He gives me new strength. How God lifts me up. God is bigger than any pp&s. I chose joy. I laughed. I mean what is more funny than being strangled by your own necklace and ear bud cords? I said no in the face of the joy stealers, and laughed, and sent those joy stealers running. I chose joy that day, and even more than that, I chose God's joy, for it is His joy that fills my soul, and brings music to my lips.

> We were filled with laughter and we sang for joy. (Psalm 126:2a)

There comes a time in everyone's life and ministry when they must reexamine where their time and energy is being used to further God's Kingdom. For those dealing with chronic illness the time to reexamine your ministry options is sometimes taken out of your hands. In addition to other ministries I was director of Vacation Bible School at my home church for many years. The time came when due to health concerns it became obvious, even to me, that I was unable to continue in this ministry. The joy stealers were just waiting to come in and steal my joy. Steal the joy from all the years I had worked for the Lord, and all the joy I had received from the kids that had come through the Vacation Bible School program. I worked with a wonderful team of volunteers over the years and this was an awesome ministry serving God and our community. Joy stealers know just where to hit us, where we are the most vulnerable. They tried stealing my joy by telling me I was not good enough to serve in this ministry anymore and no one wanted me in this ministry anyway. We can choose to wade through the mud or we can trust in Jesus and with new strength we will soar high on wings like eagles.

Joy stealers are really only effective if we give up and let them in. If we stand firm and remember who we are in Jesus Christ, if we remember that Jesus Christ not only stands with us He is our strength and our shield, we will turn to the joy stealers and tell them, "No I am not letting you steal my joy!"

One effective way I have learned to live joyfully after a life change is I seek to fill the empty space left with a new ministry or activity. joy stealers love to dwell in "empty spaces" in our lives. At one point in my life I had to hang up my baseball glove. (I would say hang up my baseball shoes but I was the slowest runner you have ever seen). Guitar lessons soon filled the space in my life that sports used to occupy. Filling the empty space left the joy stealers no room to come in. Jesus was there right beside me as I had to make this life change, one of my Christian friends gave me guitar lessons, and oh, the joy that has filled my life because I did not let the joy stealers steal my joy.

Jesus is the Life Changer. When a ministry changes, when a situation in your life changes, when a door closes Jesus will open another door. Different does not have to be worse. Different does not have to be bad. When we give our life to the life changer one thing is for certain and that is that He has your best interest in mind.

> We know that God causes everything to work together
> for the good of those who love God and are called
> according to His purpose for them. (Romans 8:28)

God loves us and causes everything to work together for our good-when we love God. When we love God and seek to walk in His ways. What joy! That God causes everything to work together for our good. There are always changes in our lives, some are small changes, some are more major changes, and Jesus will always walk with us through every change. Was there sadness involved in giving up a ministry that I had been involved in for many years? Yes, there was sadness, but when God is there closing a door He is also there opening a new door. One of the problems when we let the joy stealers in to steal our joy is that we are often also blinded to the "new joy" that God has planned for our life. Joy stealers put blinders on us when they steal our joy making it so we focus only on the fact that our joy is gone and we are then unable to see beyond the joylessness to the joy God has for us. The joy stealers love to not only steal our joy but also keep us from receiving the joy God has planned for us.

When a life change occurs we must remember, "We know God causes everything to work together for the good of those who love God." "We know." Those are words of Scripture to remember. We know. Write those words on your heart for those times when a life change happens or a lemon storm comes. And remember that God has your back and He not only will send those Joy Stealers running, He has New Joy planned for your life. What joy!

THOUGHTS ON LIVING JOYFULLY:

Isaiah 40:31 — The author says, "I cannot help but praise the Lord and thank Him for the strength he gives for each new day." When was the last time you praised the Lord and thanked Him for each new day? What were the circumstances of that day? When we leave our problems in God's hands our joy is complete and the joy stealers are unable to steal our joy. When it comes to leaving your problems in God's hands do you find it easy or difficult to do this?

Have you ever considered some of the routine things you do, such as reading the Bible, daily prayer, and being confident Jesus is always by your side, and will never leave you or forsake you as being aids you can use when you are going through a, "Lemon Storm"?

The author says, "A lemon storm is one of the joy stealers, while we are in the middle of the storm it is very hard to hang on to our joy. That is one reason it is so important to keep to our, "training routine", so that when the storm comes and all we can see is lemons falling everywhere our, "training", will kick in and our joy will bubble to the surface. Our joy will see those baskets of lemons and laugh and respond by saying, "I have Jesus, and lemons do not affect my joy. God is by my side."

A Lemon storm can be any series of problems that keep coming and coming. When have you experienced this, and how did you handle the, "storm" — both emotionally and spiritually?

The author describes having a super, very bad, yucky day. (svbyd). The author uses several things to help overcome these types of days. What do you do to help you overcome these types of days?

> Don't you realize that your body is the temple of the Holy Spirit, who lives in you and was given to you by God? You do not belong to yourself, for God bought you with a high price. So you must honor God with your body. (I Corinthians 6:19–20)

Take a few moments and contemplate that we are God's Temple. We are God's beautiful, magnificent, God-designed temple. Each of us has a Most Holy Place. God is waiting to come in and reside inside, all you have to do is ask Him to come into your life.

The author says, "The more we focus on God the bigger God becomes in our lives and the more insignificant our pain, problem, or situation, (pp&s), becomes. Do you have a difficult time keeping your eyes on God and not on your pain, problem, or situation, (pp&s)?

The author wrote about a time when a situation in the pool put her in the position where she could either choose to allow the joy stealers in or she could choose joy. Consider a time when you were in such a position and what choice you made. Would you make the same choice today? Why or Why not.

There comes a time in everyone's life and ministry when they must reexamine where their time and energy is being used to further God's Kingdom. Have you examined your ministry options? What were the results? Have you changed where your time and energy is being used? If you have not reexamined your ministry options, is it time to do so? Why or Why not.

> When a life change occurs we must remember, "We know God causes everything to work together for the good of those who love God." (Romans 8:28)

"We know"! How certain are you that God causes everything to work together for the good of those who love God? Do you say with the voice of faith, I know!

CHAPTER SIX

Pass the gravy

Look! I stand at the door and knock. If you hear my voice and open the door, I will come in, and we will share a meal together as friends. (Rev. 3:20)

When I was a kid I grew up near a supermarket and on Saturdays friends and family from near and far would come to "town" to shop at this supermarket. More times than not, either before their shopping trip or after, they would make their way to my parents' house to visit. Knocking on the door and calling "Yoo-hoo" on Saturdays was a normal occurrence. My mother never knew how many people to plan for supper on Saturdays, because she just fed whoever was at her house and was hungry. If you were at my mom's house you were welcome to eat at her table. She learned this valuable lesson from her mother. I remember many a holiday meal at my grandmother's house where unexpected guests were at her table. If you had nowhere to celebrate the holiday my grandmother would be sure to invite you to share the meal at her table. You see, there is value in coming together and sharing a meal. Coming together, sitting down, and passing food to one another says something about our feelings for one another. Fellowship is important and sharing our lives with one another is a vital part of Christian growth.

As Christians, when we gather together, whether it is just 2 or 3 or a larger group, we form a bond together that makes it difficult for the joy stealers to penetrate. We are stronger together. When we are joined together at a common meal, we acknowledge those at the table with us, are deserving of this food and nourishment that we are passing to them. That acknowledgment leads to the knowledge and acceptance that each person at the table is loved by God. The awareness and acceptance that Jesus died for everyone at the table. This knowledge brings a closeness and bond to the shared meal. You may come to the table as strangers but with God at the head of your table you will walk away rejoicing as "friends".

> By this time they were nearing Emmaus and the end of their journey. Jesus acted as if he were going on, but they begged him, "stay the night with us, since it is getting late." So he went home with them. As they sat down to eat, Jesus took the bread and blessed it. Then he broke it and gave it to them. Suddenly, their eyes were opened, and they recognized him. (Luke 24:28–31)

Two of Jesus followers were walking to the village of Emmaus, which was a good day's walk from Jerusalem. These disciples had left Jerusalem earlier in the day with very heavy hearts. Over the last few days their Lord and Master Jesus Christ had been arrested, convicted and crucified. It appears from reading the account in Luke 24:13–34 that these disciples are now returning to their homes in Emmaus. I can so relate to these disciples. When I am hurting and the joy stealers have come and stolen my joy I only wish to be home. When Jesus was going to the cross in Jerusalem the joy stealers were very busy. As we read the Gospel accounts of the last week of Jesus's life on earth, and after the Crucifixion, we see most, if not all, the disciples appear to have been visited by the joy stealers. When the joy stealers come we may want the comfort of gathering with friends and family. Have you ever been on vacation, away from home, and become ill? When this happens, no matter how fabulous the vacation locale, you really want to return home to recuperate and return to good health.

Whatever the reason that brought these followers of Christ on the road to Emmaus that day, one thing was for sure and that was that there was a divine appointment waiting for them between Jerusalem and Emmaus.

> As they walked along they were talking about everything that had happened. As they talked and discussed these things, Jesus himself suddenly came and began walking with them. But God kept them from recognizing him. (Luke 24:14–16)

These verses tell us the disciples were talking together as they walked the road to Emmaus. The news they were discussing was both grief filled and heart wrenching. As they continued talking about the things that had taken place in Jerusalem, in the previous few days, I wonder if the joy stealers had come and left the fog of confusion and despair behind. Many things can leave us with a fogginess that leaves us concentrating mostly on ourselves with very little able to penetrate through the "cloud of fog" that we have become enshrouded in. Pain, grief, sorrow, loneliness, depression, job-loss, and many others will leave us unable to recognize Jesus. We are like the disciples on the road to Emmaus, so wrapped up in ourselves and what is happening to us that we are unable to recognize the Risen Savior when He is walking step in step with us.

> By this time they were nearing Emmaus and the end of their journey. Jesus acted as if he were going on, but they begged him, "Stay the night with us, since it is getting late." So he went home with them. As they sat down to eat, he took the bread and blessed it. Then he broke it and gave it to them. Suddenly, their eyes were opened, and they recognized him. (Luke 24:28–31a)

After traveling all day together the disciples ask, (well, ok – beg) their traveling companion, whom they still have not recognized, to stay with them. As they begin to partake of the meal, Jesus takes the Bread and breaks it and blesses it. As soon as Jesus does this action the fog is lifted and the disciples recognize him. They recognize him in the meal, in the breaking of the bread, and in the blessing. Where do we see Jesus? Do we see Jesus in the gathering around the table? In the holding of hands in prayer? In the passing of the bread? Pass the bread and see Jesus in the face of your sister and your brother. Gather together and share a meal, and like the disciples on the road to Emmaus, your fog of selfishness will lift, take a moment to look around and see Jesus, he is just waiting to send those joy stealers running.

> Jesus entered Jericho and made his way through the town. There was a man there named Zacchaeus. He was the chief tax collector in the region, and he had become very rich. He tried to get a look at Jesus, but he was too short to see over the crowd. So he ran ahead and climbed a sycamore-fig tree beside the road, for Jesus was going to pass that way. When Jesus came by, he looked up at Zacchaeus and called him by name. "Zacchaeus!" he said "Quick, come down! I must be a guest in your home today." Zacchaeus quickly climbed down and took Jesus to his house in great excitement and joy. (Luke 19:1–6)

Jesus comes to Jericho and makes his way through the town because he has a divine appointment to keep. He is meeting with Zacchaeus, even though Zacchaeus does not know it yet. As Jesus is making his way through Jericho, Zacchaeus is doing everything he can to be able to see Jesus. The very first obstacle Zacchaeus encounters, as he seeks to see Jesus, is that he is rather challenged in the height department. As he tries to look over and through the crowd to see if Jesus is passing by, he is too short to see him. The scripture text tells us that Zacchaeus was the chief tax collector in that region and had become very rich. The chief tax collector leased the region from the Romans and was given authority to collect taxes in that area. The chief tax collector then over saw tax collectors under him from whom he collected a commission. This is one way Zacchaeus became very rich. The chief tax collectors were hated even more than the tax collectors under them as they were thought of as traitors for helping the Romans.

As I see Zacchaeus trying hard to look through the crowd to see if Jesus is passing by, at first I find myself surprised that the crowd is not more accommodating in helping this height challenged person. Nearly everyone in the crowd that day was looking to see Jesus, yet no one was willing to help Zacchaeus. Then, I remember how the people felt concerning tax collectors. Tax collectors were hated and despised. I also am amazed that Zacchaeus did not let those joy stealers come and steal his joy at the possibility of seeing Jesus. This is a crowd of joy stealers for sure. He is pressed on all sides by the crowd of people who dislike him and some who detest him and hate him, joy stealers all around him.

Zacchaeus had to overcome two obstacles: 1. Challenged in the height department and 2. Attacked by the joy stealers when the people of the town remind him of how they hated him. At this point Zacchaeus has a decision to make, he can continue in his quest to see Jesus or give in to the joy stealers and give up on his desire to see Jesus. Verse 4 of our Scripture in the Gospel of Luke tells us Zacchaeus, "runs", (not walks, runs!) ahead and climbs a tree so he has a better view of Jesus passing by. Zacchaeus could have run home instead of running to Jesus. Zacchaeus could have given in to the joy stealers and hung his head and turned and went home. How many times have we missed opportunities to see our Lord and Savior because we have listened to the joy stealers tell us, "You are not good enough", and we have run home instead of running to Jesus? Or how many times have we been afraid to hear what the joy stealers had to say? So we left without meeting Jesus or left without even hearing what the joy stealers had to say, just because we were afraid? Zacchaeus said no to the joy stealers and he ran to Jesus. What better place to run to then the strong arms of the One who loves us. Zacchaeus does not appear to hesitate. He just takes off running. Running to get ahead of the crowd. Running perhaps to get away from the crowd, but he is running in the right direction, not towards home but towards his appointment with Jesus. When we are surrounded on all sides, often our fight or flight reaction takes hold, and if you are anything like me, flight often wins. The joy stealers are very good at sending fear and confusion our way. When this happens where do we run? Do we run to Jesus? Do we, like Zacchaeus, turn our backs on the joy stealers and run to Jesus, or do we run and hide? Zacchaeus said no to the joy stealers, no you will not steal my joy, and he ran and climbed a sycamore tree. (Sycamore trees were well known for their ease of climbing with a short trunk and wide branches.) And there Zacchaeus waits for his divine appointment with Jesus. We do not know how long Zacchaeus had to wait in the Sycamore tree, but I get the feeling from reading about Zacchaeus that he was making himself comfortable in that tree as he waited for Jesus.

> I waited patiently for the Lord to help me and he turned
> to me and heard my cry. (Psalm 40:1)

Zacchaeus waited patiently for the Lord. We live in a world today of many "instant" things. Why should I wait for my food? Isn't this fast food? Cook in the microwave or is there something faster now? "Wait" is not in our vocabulary any longer. We are used to living in the fast lane now. Yet even in this, "everything now", time we are living in, God's voice speaks quietly yet directly, "Be still, and know that I am God! Psalm 46:10. Be still; wait. Oh, how we dislike inaction! We are a people of action, oh that we would be more like Zacchaeus and wait for our Lord.

> When Jesus came by, he looked up at Zacchaeus and
> called him by name. "Zacchaeus! He said. "Quick, come
> down! I must be a guest in your home today."(Luke 19:5)

This is a moment of great joy for Zacchaeus. Jesus knows his name! What joy! And he wants to be a guest in his house. Jesus wants to come and spend time in Zacchaeus house, eat in his house, fellowship in his house. What a beautiful thing our Savior did, He calls: Zacchaeus! In the culture of Zacchaeus day a person's name was more than just a label or identification designation. A person's name told something about their character and/or their destiny. A person's name represented their reputation and family line. For Jesus to call Zacchaeus by name was to acknowledge that Jesus knew Zacchaeus, knew who he was. I do believe if that had been me in that tree, Jesus calling my name might just have caused me to fall out of it! The joy and thrill of Jesus knowing my name might possibly have been quickly followed by the twin joy stealers of guilt and fear. Oh, No! Jesus knows my name. He knows me. What have I done?

When Jesus announces that he is going to be a guest in Zacchaeus's house that day, did he wonder if his house was in order like I would have. Did he wonder, "What will I serve the Master?" I wonder how each of us would react to Jesus declaring he was coming to our house today. With great Joy like Zacchaeus? Or with hesitation, not quite sure you want Jesus to come today? Maybe tomorrow? Maybe your house isn't ready today, or maybe you are too busy for Jesus today. Do we respond with trepidation, wondering why Jesus wants to come to our house? Jesus says he is coming to your house today, is your response, "today? Hmm, I really am not ready today, Lord." I wonder sometimes how many times the Lord offered His invitation to me before I, like Zacchaeus, said yes Lord, come into my home. How many times have I said my house is a mess and I am kind of busy today, Jesus how about next week? The scripture tells us that Zacchaeus quickly climbed down and took Jesus to his house in great excitement and joy. Quickly. No joy stealers for Zacchaeus. No hesitation for Zacchaeus. Jesus calls and he answers. Joy stealers all around him and he hears Jesus and responds. I love this story because of the lesson we learn from this height challenged, despised tax collector. Zacchaeus kept his eyes on Jesus. From the moment he decided that day to see Jesus as he passed by; his only goal was to see Jesus. He did not allow anything to deter him from his goal, no crowd of people, no joy stealers. He kept his eyes focused on Jesus and those joy stealers were sent away joyless.

> Later, Jesus appeared again to the disciples beside the Sea of Galilee. This is how it happened. Several of the disciples were there Simon Peter, Thomas, and Nathanael, from Cana in Galilee, the Sons of Zebedee, and two other disciples. Simon Peter said, "I'm going fishing". "We'll come, too," they all said. So they went out in the boat, but they caught nothing all night. At dawn Jesus was standing on the beach, but the disciples couldn't see who he was. He called out, "Fellows, have

you caught any fish?" "No." they replied. Then he said,
"Throw out your net on the right side of the boat and
you'll get some!" So they did, and they couldn't haul in
the net because there were so many fish in it. Then the
disciple Jesus loved said to Peter, "It is the Lord!" When
Simon Peter heard that it was the Lord, he put on his
tunic, (for he had stripped for work), jumped into the
water, and headed to shore. The others stayed with the
boat and pulled the loaded net to the shore, for they
were only about a hundred yards from shore. When
they got there, they found breakfast waiting for them —
fish cooking over a charcoal fire, and some bread. "Bring
some of the fish you've just caught." Jesus said. So Simon
Peter went aboard and dragged the net to the shore.
There were 153 large fish, and yet the net hadn't torn.
"Now come and have some breakfast!" Jesus said. (John
21:1–12)

I grew up in a fishing family. I learned to love fishing at a young age.
When I was growing up I loved that thrill of catching a fish. I think my
love of the beach began way back there on the shores of the, "Little Lake"
fishing for Bluegills. I came to appreciate how relaxing fishing is and how
stress free it is, sitting on the bank of the river watching the water rush
by with a fishing pole in my hand. Each spring we would look forward
to the opening of Trout Season. This date was anticipated and circled
on our calendar. There are many ways to determine when spring has
arrived, but in my family the only true way was when the circled date
of the opening of Trout Season had arrived. As so often happens in life I
drifted away from my fishing roots only to be reintroduced to them again
in the most amazing way. Several summers ago I was on vacation with
my family at a cabin on a small lake and my granddaughter would not
take, "no" to her question of, "you are going fishing with us Grandma?"
So, I found myself out on the dock, sitting in a chair, (Grandmas can fish
sitting down!) with a fishing pole in my hand. But, much to my surprise,
it is different fishing as a grandmother. Grandmothers do not have to
put their own worms on their hooks. (Yes! Their grandchildren do it for

them. Thank you grandkids.) And grandmothers do not have to take the fish off the hook. (Yes, I did catch fish, ok, a fish, but that was more than the disciples caught in our scripture verses.) I rekindled my love for fishing during that vacation and the joy I found sitting on the dock surrounded by my grandchildren no joy stealers were able to take away.

> When he had finished speaking, he said to Simon (Simon Peter), "Now go out where it is deeper and let down your nets to catch some fish." "Master," Simon, replied, "we worked hard all last night and didn't catch a thing. But if you say so, I'll let the nets down again." And this time their nets were so full of fish they began to tear! Jesus replied to Simon, "Don't be afraid! From now on you'll be fishing for people." (Luke 5:4–6 10b)

These verses in the Gospel of Luke tell us that it was while Peter was fishing he first encountered Jesus. Our scripture verses in the Gospel of John tell us Peter and the disciples fished all night and caught nothing. (Very similar to Peter's first encounter with Jesus!) Jesus standing on the beach instructs them to cast their nets on the right side of the boat and they will catch some. I really love this part of the story because once again Jesus is teaching us. If we always work on the "right side", we will be successful! The disciples do as Jesus says and get a very big haul! At this their eyes are opened and they knew it was Jesus. As Peter and the disciples came to the beach where Jesus was, Jesus greets them and says to them, "Now, come and have some breakfast!" What joy! Their Lord and Savior has been waiting for them. Jesus has cooked for them and is waiting with love and grace to share a meal with them. Now that is the best way to send those joy stealers away. Sit down and share a meal together. Say I value you and I will share my food with you, I will share my life with you. By sharing a meal together we share a bond together. For Peter and the disciples there was no better joy. There is a seat at the table just waiting for you. Hear Jesus say to you, "Come and have some breakfast, sit next to me, I have been waiting for you!" That will send those joy stealers away hungry!

THOUGHTS ON LIVING JOYFULLY:

> Look! I stand at the door and knock. If you hear my voice and open the door, I will come in, and we will share a meal together as friends. (Revelation 3:20)

The author shares several examples from her family where unexpected company were welcomed at the dinner table. When in your experience have you invited last minute guests to your dinner table? What do you feel was the result of the invitation?

After the crucifixion and resurrection of Jesus, two of Jesus's followers were journeying to Emmaus. Have you ever been away from home when you suffered a pain, problem, or situation? Did you wish to return home?

Luke 19:1 the author says Jesus comes to Jericho and makes His way through the town because he has a divine appointment with Zacchaeus, even though Zacchaeus does not know it yet. Have you ever felt like you had a divine appointment with God? That God was just waiting to get your attention? When did this happen? What was the result of your meeting with God?

Luke 19:1–6 Meditate on what lengths you would go to in order to see Jesus. Then consider Jesus is a breath and a prayer away. When is the last time you prayed and talked to Jesus? Plan a daily prayer time for the next week to talk to Jesus.

If you knew Jesus was coming to your house today, would you react with joy and excitement like Zacchaeus or would you be more uncertain and hesitant, full of excuses and delaying tactics? Does the idea of Jesus coming to your house make you joyful or nervous? Explain your feelings.

John 21:2–8 Peter announces he is going fishing and several of the disciples join him. The author believes when we feel out of control and in distress we often want to return to an activity where we were feeling comfortable and in control. Contemplate for a few moments what activity you would want to return to where you would feel comfortable and in control.

When Jesus was standing on the beach the disciples could not see who he was. They had been fishing all night and had caught nothing. Times of distress or extreme sadness will keep our eyes from recognizing

Jesus. Jesus told them to throw their nets on the right side of the boat. After obeying Jesus and catching so many fish they could not haul in the net, their eyes were opened to the presence of Jesus. When was the last time you were unable to, "see", Jesus? What helped you to open your eyes to his presence?

One of the themes of this chapter is, "seeing Jesus". After reading and studying this Chapter what have you learned about keeping your eyes on Jesus?

CHAPTER SEVEN

Where did I put my map?

> To illustrate the point further, Jesus told them this story:
> "A man had two sons. The younger son told his father, 'I
> want my share of your estate now before you die. So his
> father agreed to divide his wealth between his sons. A
> few days later this younger son packed all his belongings
> and moved to a distant land, and there he wasted all his
> money in wild living. (Luke 15:11–13)

This story, that Jesus tells here, in the Gospel of Luke, begins with a
rather gentle introduction, "A man had two sons." In those days, having
2 sons was something to celebrate. Two sons almost insured the family
line would continue and the father would be taken care of in his old age.
With this introduction we understand the pride and joy the father has in
his sons. Then we read verse 12 and we see how quickly the joy stealers
make an appearance in this story. The younger son told his father, "I want
my share of your estate now before you die." (vs 12) Many of us have
also experienced feelings of pride and joy in our children one moment;
suddenly change to disappointment the next. Sometimes, being a parent
is not a job for the weak hearted. Often the joy stealers are just waiting
and watching parents so they can swoop in and steal their joy. The

younger son wants his share of the estate now before the father dies. Now here is a case of the joy stealers coming. The joy stealers try to steal all the joy this father is receiving from his two sons. Now is the time that doubt and fear try to set in for the father, wondering does my son wish I had already died? Have I out lived my usefulness? Of course, the choir of "friends", are quick to chime in with their opinions on the younger son's request.

Putting ourselves in the place of the, "Father", this just adds to our doubt and fear, making our lives more available to the joy stealers. Many of us have experienced the same feelings the father in the story may have felt. Parenting, then and now, is a journey full of ups and downs. It is a journey that comes without a guidebook and that in itself causes much difficulty. The joy stealers are excellent at what they do. But we have a truly wonderful defense against the joy stealers. Remember when doubt and fear set in, that is when we turn to the One who is our Protector.

> Those who look to Him for help will be radiant with joy; no shadow of shame will darken their faces. In my desperation I prayed, and the Lord listened; he saved me from all my troubles. For the angel of the Lord is a guard; he surrounds and defends all who fear him. (Psalms 34:5–7)

I believe the father in our story is familiar with our Protector, because we see no shame upon him as he gives in to his younger son's request. The father agrees and divides his wealth between his two sons. At this point in the story we do not know much about the older son. He has not made an appearance in our story yet. The younger son however is playing a starring role. Sometimes when we are the younger son or daughter we are the one at the, "bottom of the barrel", All the jobs trickle down to us. All the clothes get, "handed down" to us. Everyone tells us what to do. We are the youngest, the littlest. To some degree, we are able to sympathize and understand the younger son, and how he may have come to this decision. Tired of always being last, and always being told what to do by "everyone", always being the one out in the field at night watching the flock. He makes a somewhat rash and foolhardy request. A request that his father could very possibly have denied. Why would the father agree to such a request? The request was an insult to the father and showed the son had little respect for him. Yet in his love for his son, the father agrees to his son's request. A few days later the father divides his wealth between his sons, and his youngest packs up and leaves. The joy stealers did not stay away very long in our story. They are back, and they are back with a vengeance. The younger son says, "Thanks for the money," and off he goes. Does he go alone? Or off with a bunch of friends, who have been waiting for this day? Friends who have been encouraging the younger son in his desire for his inheritance. Friends who might not really be friends? We do not know the answer to these questions, as the scripture does not tell us. Either way, off he goes to a distant land where he wastes all his money on wild living. We do not have a timeline of how long it took to go through his money, but from the story I get the impression the money slipped through his fingers fairly quickly. He goes through the money, and perhaps, he goes through the friends, because we do find him alone in the distant land. It may have taken the father almost a lifetime to accumulate the money, but it did not take his son very long to spend it on wild living.

The younger son, perhaps weary of living under the rules of his father, has taken his inheritance and used it for his own pleasure. Many of us today, in an abstract way, have followed in the younger sons footsteps. Tired of responsibilities, rules, troubles, misfortunes, sorrow, etc. we have fled from our current circumstances, seeking a place of refuge to spend our, "riches". God has graced each of us with talents and abilities (i.e. riches).

> In His Grace, God has given us different gifts for doing certain things well. So if God has given you the ability to prophesy speak out with as much faith as God has given you. (Romans 12:6)

In our place of "refuge", the place we have chosen to put down roots, the place we have arrived at after saying, "I cannot wait until I can move away from here;" are we using our riches (the gifts and talents God has given us) for our own pleasures and self-promotion, or are we using those riches to serve one another, and for the advancement of the Gospel of Jesus Christ? How are we using the gifts and talents God gives us?

> God has given each of you a gift from his great variety
> of Spiritual gifts. Use them well to serve one another.
> (1 Peter 4:10)

There are days our lives resemble the younger sons in the distant land. We have left the homeland and struck out on our own because we grew weary of our lives, the joy stealers paid us a visit, and we have a better plan. Yet it did not take long in this, "distant land", to find that our plan was not really better, and that, "What!" the joy stealers are still with us. That is one of the unique characteristics of the joy stealers, they are able to follow us where ever we go. We may try to run away from them, but they follow right along, step by step with us. Stop and make a stand, remember who you belong to:

> ...now that you belong to Jesus Christ. (I Corinthians
> 1:4b)

and send those joy stealers running.

> When he finally came to his senses, he said to himself,
> "At home even the hired servants have food enough to
> spare, and here I am dying of hunger!" I will go home
> to my father and say, "father, I have sinned against both
> heaven and you, and I am no longer worthy of being
> called your son. Please take me on as a hired servant".
> (Luke 15:17–18)

The younger son was in quite the dilemma. He was starving and the only work he could find was as a hired hand working in the fields feeding the pigs. For a Jewish person this was the worst job imaginable. Pigs were unclean animals and Jewish people could not by law and rule touch them. As he stood knee deep in pig slop his heart turned to home and heaven and God turned that pig slop into the Road to Redemption. As the younger son took his first steps on the Redemption Road his father at home has been busy on his end of the Redemption Road. As the son is standing in the fields growing hungrier by the minute he begins to understand that he has been visited by joy stealers. He begins to remember who he is and who he belongs to. Luke 15:18: "I will go <u>home</u> to my father and say, 'Father I have sinned against <u>both heaven and you,</u> and I am no longer worthy of being called your son. Please take me on as a hired servant.'" (Underline added by author) The younger son stops and makes a stand.

> So he returned home to his father. And while he was still a long way off, his father saw him coming. Filled with love and compassion, he ran to his son, embraced him, and kissed him. His son said to him, "Father, I have sinned against both heaven and you, and I am no longer worthy of being called your son." But his father said to the servants, "Quick! Bring the finest robe in the house and put it on him. Get a ring for his finger and sandals for his feet. And kill the calf we have been fattening. We must celebrate with a feast, for this son of mine was dead and has now returned to life. He was lost, but now he is found. So the party began. (Luke 15:19–24)

Verse 20 tells us he returned home to his father and, "while he was still a long way off, his father saw him coming. Filled with love and compassion, he ran to his son, embraced him, and kissed him." Those joy stealers were sent away fast. There was no room for them here in this family reunion.

The father saw the son coming, "while he was still a long way off." This verse, Luke 15:20 is one of the most beautiful verses in the Bible. The younger son has been gone for a time. What that "time" is we have no idea. More than a "while". A span of time, a stretch of time, a period of time, a season of time. And during this time there has been a missing chair at the table. The father has not stopped missing his son. Verse 20 tells us how the father has longed for the sons return. Do you not see it? The father was looking for the sons return. If it was in today's world I would expect the father had his binoculars up and saw the son coming!

That is how intently the father is keeping watch for his sons return. The father is looking for the sons return because he has great faith that the son will return. He looks every day with expectation. No joy stealers here. The father knows the son will return. Even after the son left with his inheritance, the father loves, the father forgives, the father watches, the father waits for the wandering sons return. On this particular day the father is rewarded for his faithful, attentive, and patient, watching when he sees his son coming. Overcome with love for his son he did something quite unexpected for a man of his status – he ran! Yes, he ran to his son. I think nothing in this story portrays the deep feelings the father has for his son than these 2 simple words, "he ran". I wonder when the last time was that you "ran" to meet someone. I also wonder what the son thinks of his father's response to his return. I wonder if the son stopped in shocked surprise to see his father running towards him. Does this give the son a clue as to how much the father loves him? How much the father has always loved him? His feet continued on towards his father and the reunion on Redemption Road.

In verse 21 we read that the wayward son tells his father he has sinned against both heaven and him and is no longer worthy of being called his son. The son was barely able to get the words he has been rehearsing over and over, as he has traveled home, out of his mouth before his father is turning to the servants and ordering them to bring the items that would symbolize the son was reinstated as a full member in good standing of the family. The finest robe in the house, a ring for his finger, and sandals for his feet.

His father then ordered that the calf was to be killed so they could celebrate with a feast. For the son who was starving, this must have sounded like heaven. I wonder if the son was amazed by his father's actions. The joy stealers have had many perfect opportunities to steal all the joy from this family, from the beginning of, "I want my money," which really wasn't the younger son's money at all, to starving and wallowing with the pigs. Or the townspeople whispering, not so quietly, that the father's younger son is a fortune-spending, party-going, lay-a-bout, who had taken his father's money before it was due him! Added to these whisperers the joy stealers were whispering that the father was a foolish old man for agreeing to give his son his inheritance. Yes, this family had been visited by the joy stealers, and they had appeared to have settled in for a very long visit. Yet, as we read through this story we are surprised to find that this is not the case. The son, as he stood that day among the pigs, made a very important choice. He said, today, I chose joy. Part of his education would have been learning, reciting, remembering the Psalms of David. As he was choosing joy that day, he may have remembered these verses from Psalm 27.

> The Lord is my light and my salvation –so why should I be afraid? The Lord is my fortress, protecting me from danger, so why should I tremble? (Psalm 27:1)

> The one thing I ask of the Lord—the one thing I seek most—is to live in the house of the Lord all the days of my life, delighting in the Lord's perfections and meditating in his Temple. (Psalm 27:4)

The son turned his feet toward home, sent the joy stealers away and once the reunion occurred, the party began. This is the last we hear of the younger son.

Now the attention shifts to the older son. He has been out working in the fields. Unlike his father it does not appear like he has been waiting, watching, or expecting his wayward brother's return. Since the Scriptures do not tell us, we have no idea how he felt when his younger brother asked for his inheritance, and took off for party life and city living. I know how my big brother reacted when I did something dumb. I think he usually wanted to pound on me! The older son has remained faithful to the father, spending time in the field, and helping the father however he could. As he has remained home, he also has heard the joy stealer's whispers about his younger brother, "he has been hanging around with a no good crowd, he spent money on wild parties, and now he has no money left at all!" I wonder, as he saw his father watching for his brother's return, if he ever thought his brother would return home. Or, if he just thought his father was being a foolish old man, for expecting his younger son's return. On this day, as he is coming back from the fields, he is startled as he hears music coming from the house.

> Meanwhile, the older son was in the fields working.
> When he returned home he heard music and dancing
> in the house. (Luke 15:25)

What? There was a party going on that he had not been invited to!
What was going on? While he was in the field working, yes, working,
someone threw a full-blown party, with music and dancing. Now, I do
not know about you, but if I had been out in the fields working all day,
and when I came home I found a party going on full force in my house,
I might not be so happy. I would be thinking that, gee, seems like they
could have waited until I got home from work before they started the
party, they did not invite me to. Giving the older son a little credit, this
party business did get started off on the wrong foot, (so to speak). I mean
did they not notice that one of the sons was missing, again? Hey, hmm-
the older son isn't here, maybe we should wait? Well, maybe!

> And he asked one of the servants what was going on.
> Your brother is back, he was told, and your father has
> killed the fattened calf. We are celebrating because of
> his safe return. (Luke 15:26-27)

The older son asks one of the servants what the celebration was all
about. The servant fills him in on his brother's return and on his father's
throwing the party. Oh boy. The older son is not happy and refuses to
go to the party. Add the resentment that may have been building up
since his brother left, to the not-invited-to-the-party insult, and we find
this older brother vulnerable to the joy stealers.

> The older brother was angry and wouldn't go in. His
> father came out and begged him. (Luke 15:28)

The father comes out and pleads with the older son to come and
join the party. This gives the older son the opportunity to voice his
feelings. Sometimes that is all we need. The chance to say our piece and
for someone to listen.

> But he replied, "All these years I've slaved for you and
> never once refused to do a single thing you told me to.
> And in all that time you never gave me even one young
> goat for a feast with my friends. Yet when this son of
> yours comes back after squandering your money on
> prostitutes, you celebrate by killing the fattened calf!"
> (Luke 15:29-30)

The older son lays his feelings out. "All these years". Has he held
back his feelings of bitter resentment at his younger brother for years?
Verse 30 gives us a clue, when he refuses to acknowledge his relationship
to his brother but refers to him as, "this son of yours." It has been my
experience that bitterness multiplies when it is not dealt with. That
appears to be the case in this story. Verse 30 holds some true resentment
towards his brother for leaving and squandering the "father's" money
on prostitutes. And at the father for honoring him with a celebration.
When the father and the younger son had a visit from the joy stealers
they both had their faith to fall back on to fight against them. When the
older son had a visit from the joy stealers he fell back on feelings and
resentments both old and new, and these were not good "tools" to use
in the battle against them.

> "His father said to him, 'Look, dear son, you have always
> stayed by me, and everything I have is yours. We had
> to celebrate this happy day. For your brother was dead
> and has come back to life! He was lost, but now he is
> found!" (Luke 5:31-32)

The father loves his son, both sons. In verse 31 he addresses his
oldest son as dear son. The joy stealers have another attack planned
and put into action. His youngest son has returned home and now his
oldest son is withdrawing. That is a perfect, joy stealer plan. But not
for this faith grounded son-loving father. Not a chance. He tells his
son, "Everything I have is yours". "But, we had to celebrate this happy
day." Celebrate! Be joyful! Do not let the joy stealers in. Celebrate! Your

brother walked Redemption Road, he has returned, that will send those joy stealers back to the pig farm!

This story that Jesus told has many twists and turns. As I have read through this scripture many times during my Christian journey I have at different stages of my life identified with each of the persons in the story. As a parent I have related to the father in the story who loves his sons. I can so understand waiting and watching for a wayward child's return. A parent's love is deep and strong. Yet there is nothing that cuts deeper than a child's words; "I want my money now." When we open ourselves to love deeply, we also open ourselves to hurt deeply. When the wayward child leaves, we, like the father in the story, wait and watch and listen, (for the phone to ring). We love, we wait, and like the father in the story, we forgive.

I have identified with the faithful son many times, as I can understand his feelings as he returned from the fields. Who wants to find a party going on that they were not invited to? But as we consider the faithful son, we find he had issues going back a ways. Well, I guess I do, too. This son needs the father's love. The story ends with the father giving his love but without us knowing if the faithful son accepts the fathers love. We do not know the end of this part of the story.

The wayward son is the focus of a lot of the story. I do not have to think very hard to identify with the wayward son. There are times that we grow weary of where God has us, for one reason or another, and we pick up, take our inheritance and move on, (physically, emotionally, spiritually, or mentally). God has us where he want us, where he needs us, and we say no thank you, not here, I am moving on. We do our best to run away from our responsibilities and soon we find ourselves standing in the pig slop, praying, "I have sinned against my Father in Heaven", and we begin our walk on Redemption Road. Ever thankful we have a Father in Heaven who loves us, who watches for us, who waits for us, who forgives us and who has provided a Redemption Road for us.

In our Scripture story, the father represents God, our loving Heavenly Father. The wayward son represents those who are, "lost" and/or have turned away from God, and the faithful son represents the religious leaders and Pharisees. The wonderful fact that it is Jesus who is telling this story stands out. It is Jesus who tells us of the father's love, of the father's forgiveness. Who would know more about the fathers love than his son? Who would know more about Redemption than the One sent to redeem the World? When the wayward son began the journey, from pig slop to forgiveness, on the Redemption road, were his steps slow, or did he hurry along the road towards home? One thing is for sure, there was no way those joy stealers were welcome on the Redemption Road!

THOUGHTS ON LIVING JOYFULLY:

Luke 15:11–13 - A man had two sons. The author states - many of us have also experienced feelings of pride and joy in our children one moment suddenly change to disappointment the next. Contemplate a time your children turned your joy to disappointment.

Psalm 34:5–7 - The author says, "I believe the father is familiar with our Protector because we see no shame upon him as he gives in to his younger son's request. Have you ever felt God was with you as you made an unpopular decision that you were certain was the right (God approved) decision? Are you the youngest in your family? If yes, did you feel some of the emotions described by the author? If you were not the youngest can you understand some of the feelings of the youngest or do you feel the youngest is just spoiled?

The younger son says thanks for the money and off he goes. The author says, "It may have taken the father almost a lifetime to accumulate the money, but it did not take his son very long to spend it on wild living." If you were the father how would you feel toward your wayward son upon hearing he was spending all his, (your) money? Would you be ready to see him again? Why or why not.

The author states, "We have followed in the younger sons footsteps. Tired of responsibilities….we have fled from our current circumstances, seeking a place of refuge to spend our "riches". Spend some time contemplating the difference from your place of refuge and the place you started out from. Do you believe God was with you on your journey and as you settled into your place of refuge? Are you using your riches for God's Glory?

Luke 15:17–18 - The younger son has spent every dime and the only job available is the worst job ever. Have you ever been in that position?

Did you take the job or ask for help? Why or why not. The author says, "As he stood knee deep in pig slop his heart turned to home and heaven and God turned that pig slop into the Road to Redemption. God can prepare the way but we must make the 1st step. Do you remember when you made your 1st steps on the Road to Redemption? Take a moment and thank God for his saving Grace.

The father saw the son coming, "While he was still a long way off." The author says Luke 15:20 is one of the most beautiful verses in the Bible. The father has never stopped missing and loving his son. What do you think the younger son thought when he saw his father running towards him? How do you think he felt when the father reinstates him as a full member in good standing in the family? Even to the point of throwing a feast for him.

What would you think and feel if you came home from work one day and found there was a party going on in your back yard? Luke 5:31-32 The father gave an explanation to the older son when he found out the older son was not coming to the party. If you were the son would you understand and join the celebration in honor of your brother?

Which person in this story do you identify with?

CHAPTER EIGHT

Have you seen my neighbor?

For many years I as a member of the worship committee of my home church. One of the reasons I so enjoyed being a member of this committee was the worship committee helped plan special services and events for our congregation. Joining with others to plan spiritual services to help draw people closer to Jesus brought me great joy. Another duty of the worship committee was maintaining the sanctuary and the altar. This also was an exciting experience. Over the years it was a blessing to become knowledgeable about the Christian church calendar and the seasons of the church year. Many things are involved in the church year – symbols, colors, special dates. The worship committee often decorates the altar at my home church according to the church calendar. The worship committee often plans 2 to 3 months ahead of the actual calendar. It is a very rewarding committee to be a member of and it was a very sad day when due to health concerns it was necessary for me to step down from this committee. Our churches, our church sanctuaries are very important, holy places; set apart for the praise and worship of our Heavenly Father. I am thankful for those who give of their time to serve on the committees who care for our holy sanctuaries.

My illness affects my ability to handle stress, I have often said, "I do not remember how well I handled stress before, (you know, the "before") my health crisis, but I sure know I do not handle stress at all now!" At the time I chose to step down from the worship committee I was dealing with some additional personal problems, which became just too much for my body to handle. People with chronic illness deal with so many things that affect our abilities to cope, not only with our bodies, but with life in general. Simple things like deciding what to wear can become major obstacles. Stress is a paralyzing problem. As we are stuck in stress mode, the joy stealers take the opportunity to attack us with everything they have. I experienced this when I stepped down from the worship committee. It was difficult to see a ministry that I had loved and been a part of for so long come to an end, but I knew that God was watching over me, and that He would carry me through, and send those joy stealers packing. When we are weak and stressed, God is always there for us.

> And the Holy Spirit helps us in our weakness. For example, we don't know what God wants us to pray for. But the Holy Spirit prays for us with groaning's that cannot be expressed in words. (Romans 8:26)

When we are in the grip of stress induced paralysis, and even the simplest decisions seem monumental, we can send those joy stealers away, because when we do not even know what to pray for, the Holy Spirit steps in for us, and prays with groaning's that cannot be expressed in words. God, and the Holy Spirit look out for us, no joy stealers can stand against them!

In the Jewish tradition it was the Levites, descendants of Levi, who took care of the Temple and all the holy furnishings in the Temple, (basins, pitchers, dishes, candles, incense, etc.) Our scripture is from the Gospel of Luke and involves a Levite and a Priest.

> One day an expert in religious law stood up to test Jesus by asking him this question: "Teacher, what should I do to inherit eternal life?" Jesus replied, "What does the law of Moses say? How do you read it?" The man answered, "'You must love the Lord your God with all your heart,

all your soul, all your strength, and all your mind.' And, 'Love your neighbor as yourself.'" "Right!" Jesus told him. "Do this and you will live!"

The man wanted to justify his actions, so he asked Jesus, "And who is my neighbor?" Jesus replied with a story: "A Jewish man was traveling from Jerusalem down to Jericho, and he was attacked by bandits. They stripped him of his clothes, beat him up, and left him half dead beside the road. By chance a priest came along. But when he saw the man lying there, he crossed to the other side of the road and passed him by. A temple assistant walked over and looked at him lying there, but he also passed by on the other side. (Luke 10:25–32)

An expert in religious law has been talking to Jesus and in the course of the discussion he finds himself on the losing side of the discussion. The expert asks Jesus what to do to inherit eternal life.

"You must love the Lord your God with all your heart, all your soul, all your strength, and all your mind, and love your neighbor as yourself." (Luke 10:27)

Apparently the religious leader wanted to be sure what the parameters were for deciding who his neighbors were, so he asks Jesus, "Who is my neighbor?"

When I was growing up I had no trouble figuring out who was my neighbor, because everyone in the neighborhood was my neighbor. Even the lady who kept all our baseballs when they were hit and landed in her fenced-in yard. Oh yes, the joy stealers were very active even back then, but God was with me even then filling me with joy each day. I grew up in the inner city and we played baseball in the street, as there was nowhere else to play. We also played "hide and seek" most evenings. As day turned to dusk, it was common for us kids to hide wherever we could. Someone stepping out on their porch might find a neighbors child, "hiding" there. A wink and a smile from the adult, and the child would know their hiding spot was safe. That is how it was in my neighborhood when I was growing up, the adults not only looked out for their children, they also looked-out for all the children. This created a perception of a safe and secure environment to grow up in. This taught me that my neighbors were the people around me and taking care of each other was part of being a good neighbor.

Jesus answered the religious leaders question with a story. Luke 10:30, tells us a Jewish man was traveling from Jerusalem down to Jericho, and he was attacked by bandits. The road the Jewish man was traveling was a popular route, between the two bustling towns. Jerusalem was where the Jewish Temple was. Jews went there to offer sacrifices, worship, and gather during festivals. Jerusalem was also a center of commerce and trade. The Jewish man was traveling to Jericho, which was also a prosperous city. Not as large as Jerusalem, it also was a successful city of commerce and trade. The road between the two cities was a common route taken and the dangers of the road were also well known. Thieves and bandits were aware of the many travelers on the road and would lie and wait for unaware travelers. Therefore, for safety reasons many people chose to travel in groups or caravans for protection. The road was a winding, twisting difficult route, and was very easy for unscrupulous people to hide in wait for unsuspecting travelers. The Jewish man in the story Jesus tells us was traveling alone, against common social practice of the day, and was attacked by bandits, and left lying on the side of the road, "half dead". Now the Scriptures do not tell us anymore about his condition, if he was conscious, or if he was making any sounds. Only that they beat him up, and left him half dead beside the road. Now, I am thankful that the bandits left him beside the road where he would easily be found, as is the case in the Scripture.

> By chance a priest came along. But when he saw the man lying there, He crossed to the other side of the road and passed him by. A temple assistant walked over and looked at him lying there, but he also passed by on the other side. (Luke 10:31–32)

By chance a priest came along. In the Jewish tradition a priest was a descendant of Aaron, from the tribe of Levi. Priests served in the Temple and offered sacrifices to God, represented the people before God, and served as a judge in cases of dispute. A priest was traveling the same road as the Jewish man. When he saw the man lying there he crossed to the other side of the road. This verse is a little startling. We would expect someone traveling, seeing a fellow traveler in desperate need would rush to help, not rush to the opposite side of the road. My husband and I travel a little, and we have found that travelers as a rule rely on each other as they are all far from home, and sometimes in a foreign country. Apparently this priest did not feel any, "traveler loyalty" as he hustled across the street.

In accordance with Jewish religious law, if a priest touched a dead body he would become "unclean" for seven days. During these seven days he would be unable to enter the Temple or perform any of his priestly duties. This may be one of the reasons he moved to the other side of the road as soon as he saw the man lying there and passed him by. In some respects I think we hold priests (and pastors) to a higher standard. If anyone would stop and give aid in this situation, we think, it would be a priest. So it shocks us, when the priest sees the man and crosses the road and leaves the poor man lying there. Yes, if he touched him, the priest may have been made unclean, but, a minor inconvenience to save a life. We are shocked yes, until we look in the mirror and ask how many times have I been "the priest"? Seeing, without even looking at our fellow man. Too busy, too important, to stop and help our fellow traveler, on this journey called life. When have I been the "priest", and have not stopped and spoken the Words of Life to someone beaten down by life and left half dead at my roadside? When have I looked and not seen, and crossed over and passed by, when the words of John 3:16 may have begun the healing and life renewing process?

Verse 32 tells us a temple assistant, (a Levite), also came by and walked over and looked at the man lying there. The temple assistant unlike the priest actually walked over and looked at the half dead Jewish man lying beside the road. Even so, he like the priest, crossed to the other side of the road, and left him lying there by the side of the road. Once again, while reading this Scripture we find ourselves a bit shocked that here is another person, a temple assistant, for us someone we would see as active in church ministry, walking past, instead of stopping and giving aid to his fellow man. When the temple assistant looked at the beaten man, we wonder what he saw, and how he came to the decision to pass him by. We too, make that kind of decision, sometimes on a daily basis. People with many wounds and burdens, we look at and then pass by. How do we come to that decision, to pass them by? Oh, we say, "we are not qualified." Or we say, "I am not the right person." I say those words come from the joy stealers. The joy stealers are just waiting for a situation such as this. For if the joy stealers can stop you from helping a wounded person, two people have had their joy stolen. Stand up to those joy stealers, remember we serve a Great God.

> For that is what God is like. He is our God forever and ever, and he will guide us until we die. (Psalm 48:14)

> I look up to the mountains, does my help come from there? My help comes from the Lord, who made heaven and earth! He will not let you stumble; the one who watches over you will not slumber. Indeed, he who watches over Israel never slumbers or sleeps. The Lord himself watches over you! The Lord stands beside you as your protective shade. (Psalm 121:1–5)

As we face situations we believe are beyond our capabilities, we must look to our Great God, who never slumbers or sleeps. What calming words from the Scriptures. The Lord himself watches over us. The words from Psalm 48 tell us He is our guide. No matter what situation we find ourselves in we will always have a helper and a guide. When we stand on those promises and turn to those joy stealers, they will be the ones crossing the road and high tailing it out of there! No joy stealers can stand against us when we are standing firm on the Word of God. Take that joy stealers!

When we look at our wounded and burdened man, now with the Word of God firmly rooted in our lives, we may see the same circumstances, but I believe our decision process, and decision outcome, will be different. Now our hope is in God, not in ourselves, our hearts fill with joy as in Psalm 126:3, "Yes, the Lord has done amazing things for us!" What joy!

> Then a despised Samaritan came along and when he saw the man, he felt compassion for him. Going over to him, the Samaritan soothed his wounds with olive oil and wine and bandaged them. Then he put the man on his own donkey and took him to an inn, where he took care of him. The next day he handed the innkeeper 2 silver coins, telling him, 'Take care of this man. If his bill runs higher than this, I'll pay you the next time I'm here'. (Luke 10:33–35)

After the temple assistant left, a Samaritan came along and he stopped to look at the man beaten and half-dead beside the road. When the Samaritan looks at the man he felt compassion for him. A Samaritan! Jews and Samaritans hated each other. This long established conflict began in 721 BC, when many Jews were captured and carried away into captivity by the Assyrians. The Assyrians then repopulated Israel with people from Gentile cities. These foreigners intermarried with the Israelite population that was still around Samaria. Because the Israelite inhabitants of Samaria had intermarried with the foreigners they adopted their idol worship. When the Jews returned from captivity and discovered these "Samaritans", their new marital status, and the idol worship altars that had been built in their absence, this was the beginning of the long standing feud. The Samaritans felt they had stayed behind and had taken care of the land and because of this felt a certain amount of ownership and did not appreciate the Jews coming back and pronouncing judgment on them. Of course over the years other issues arose that just added fuel to the fire that became irreconcilable differences.

When we read verse 33 and see a despised Samaritan came along and felt compassion for our Jewish man who was attacked by bandits, well, now we are shocked again. Jesus has been surprising us with this story verse by verse! Our Jewish traveler, attacked by bandits and lying half-dead on the side of the road, I think if we could ask for someone to come by to help him it might be a priest. No, that did not work. A temple worker. Oh, that did not work either. How about the people who do not like us, and we do not like them, let's send one of them? Only by the Grace of God. Because when the Samaritan sees the wounded Jew lying there he soothed his wounds and bandaged them. And then he even goes the extra mile by putting the Jewish man on his donkey and taking him to an Inn where he takes care of him. I see such a difference from our priest and temple assistant and the Samaritan. I think the Samaritan has Psalm 106 in his mind and joy in his heart.

> Praise the LORD! Give thanks to the LORD, for he is good! His faithful love endures forever. Who can list the glorious miracles of the LORD? Who can ever praise him enough? There is joy for those who deal justly with others and always do what is right. (Psalm 106:1–3)

The Samaritan dealt justly with the wounded Jewish man. As he felt compassion for his fellow man, yes, for his neighbor, he acted first by soothing and bandaging his wounds, and then by putting him on his own donkey and taking him to an Inn, to take care of him.

Who was the Jewish man's neighbor? That is the question Jesus asks the expert in religious law, and the question he asks each of us. Yes, we are surprised and shocked, at the actions of the priest and the temple assistant, but are we surprised and shocked by the actions, when we are the ones "crossing the road". Do we find ourselves singing with joy in our hearts, as Psalm 106:3 says: "There is joy for those who deal justly with others, and always do what is right." Or are we fighting the joy stealers as we "cross the road" and leave a "neighbor" without the aid he so desperately needs? Psalm 106:3 does not say sometimes do what is right, or part of the time do what is right. It says, "Always do what is right"! There is a reason our Bibles do not come with a bottle of whiteout. We cannot change the Bible to fit our needs or wishes.

> The grass withers and the flowers fade, but the word of our God stands forever. (Isaiah 40:8)

God's word remains the same forever. It is righteous and true.

> For the word of God is alive and powerful. It is sharper
> than the sharpest two-edged sword, cutting between
> soul and spirit, between joint and marrow. It exposes our
> innermost thoughts and desires. Nothing in all creation
> is hidden from God. Everything is naked and exposed
> before His eyes, and He is the one to whom we are
> accountable. (Hebrews 4:12–13)

The word of God not only stands, it is alive and powerful. Nothing is hidden from God. When we, like the priest and the temple assistant, leave our neighbor lying in the dusty road in need of aid, our actions are exposed before God's eyes. I know when I have been the one crossing the road, the joy stealers are very busy taking that opportunity to slip in and steal my joy. My defenses are down because I am busy "making excuses as to why it was a good idea to leave my neighbor lying in the dusty road in need of aid". Of course, there was no excuse. As I crossed the road, I missed the opportunity to serve Jesus. Many times each day we are presented with the opportunity to serve Jesus. We can say yes to the opportunity, and step forward in the love of Christ and help our neighbor, or we can say no, and miss the opportunity to spread the love of Christ.

> And the King will say, 'I tell you the truth, when you did
> it to one of the least of these my brothers and sisters, you
> were doing it to me!' (Matthew 25:40)

This verse, in the Gospel of Matthew, reminds us that what we do to others, we are in actuality doing to our Lord. When we walk the road between Jerusalem and Jericho and turn our back on the man who was beaten up and left half dead on the side of the road, we are turning our back on our Lord Jesus Christ. When we refuse to help care for the wounds on the half-dead man, we are refusing to care for Jesus's wounds. This gives us a different perspective as we walk that dusty road.

Who is my neighbor? Does my neighbor wear the face of Christ?

The Samaritan took quick action, he first felt compassion, then soothed his wounds. Next he took the man to an Inn where he was taken care of. Unlike the priest and the temple worker, who also took quick action by crossing the road and leaving the Jewish man lying half-dead by the side of the road. We are left with the question, who is our neighbor? How do we respond? Do we listen to the joy stealers and quickly cross the road leaving the injured man lying by the side of the road? Or do we listen to God and send those joy stealers across the road alone and let joy abound in us, and in the injured man, as we tend to his wounds? Take that joy stealers, we know who our neighbors are! Our neighbors are those in need of the love of Jesus Christ; we are His ambassadors, willing to share His love with the whole world.

> Imitate God, therefore, in everything you do, because you are his dear children. Live a life filled with love, following the example of Christ. He loved us and offered himself as a sacrifice for us, a pleasing aroma to God. (Ephesians 5:1-2)

Imitate Jesus, I can think of no one better to pattern my life after. Jesus knew who his neighbor was.

> I will not judge those who hear me but don't obey me, for I have come to save the world and not to judge it. (John 12:47)

Jesus came to save the world! The world was Jesus's neighbor! As we imitate Jesus, and live a life filled with love, we share that love with those around us, our neighbors. Believe me, those joy stealers will be sent away quickly, as our neighbors are celebrating with love and joy.

THOUGHTS ON LIVING JOYFULLY:

Romans 8:26 – The author says when we are in the grip of stress induced paralysis, and even the simplest decisions seem monumental, we can send those joy stealers away, because when we do not even know what to pray for, the Holy Spirit steps in and prays for us. Meditate on the idea of the Holy Spirit praying for you. Does this bring you comfort? Why or why not. Luke 10:29–32 – Who is my neighbor? A Jewish man is journeying to Jericho and he is attacked by bandits and left half dead on the side of the road. A priest comes by but when he sees the injured man he crosses to the other side of the road and leaves the injured man lying there. Are you surprised the priest did not help the injured Jewish man? Why or why not? A temple assistant walked over and looked at the injured man lying there, but he also left him lying there. Are you surprised the temple assistant did not help the injured Jewish man? Why or why not? Luke 10:33–37 - Then a despised Samaritan came along and when he saw the injured man, he felt compassion for him. This is unusual because of the ongoing feud between the Jews and the Samaritans. Meditate on how often we let social customs stop us from reaching out to someone in need. Who was the Jewish man's neighbor? Contemplate when the last time was you crossed the road rather than "be a neighbor" and offer aid. Spend time in prayer asking God how you can be a better neighbor.

CHAPTER NINE

A little water with my pie, please

A man named Lazarus was sick. He lived in Bethany with his sisters, Mary and Martha. This is the Mary who later poured the expensive perfume on the Lord's feet, and wiped them with her hair. Her brother Lazarus was sick. So the two sisters sent a message to Jesus telling him, "Lord, your dear friend is very sick." (John 11:1–3)

Several years ago I was shopping at our all and everything store in the toy department, as I stood in the aisle trying to decide what to buy, a football (one of those nerf foam footballs) came flying out of nowhere and plunked me on the head! After I got my brain back working, I looked around and there was no one to be found. I thought, O.K. God, now what? I know I have a difficult time listening, but He does not usually have to go to that extreme to get my attention. Recently, I was praying about a distressing situation and after praying for a time and not hearing from God, I asked Him why I had not received any word about this situation. God answered me that He would like to but, He could not get a word in because I would not quit talking! Yes, I was doing a lot of talking and forgetting to be silent and listen. Seems like when I pray, I talk to God, say my Amen, and off I am to my regular activities, never remembering to spend time in silence with my ears listening for God's voice.

There will be days when we believe we have fallen short and have disappointed ourselves and God. Perhaps we did not respond to the hurts of our neighbor as quickly as we thought we should. We hold ourselves to a very high standard. Whatever the reason, the outcome is the same, we are depressed and angry at ourselves for our actions or lack of actions, and one of the first things that begin to suffer is our prayer life. Our prayer life is our communication with God. Once our communication with God is disrupted the joy stealers take this opportunity to begin to convince us that we are worthless, that everything we do ends up in failure. It does not take long for the joy stealers to so remind us of all our short comings that we return to our couch, chair, bed, day after day. Joyless, accomplishing nothing. Because the joy stealers have convinced us that we are worthless.

As we are stuck joyless on the couch we need to turn to Jesus as our example. Jesus faced his joy stealers. Jesus knowing what lay ahead for him and that the biggest joy stealer of all, Satan, waited with a plan for his destruction, yet this did not stop Jesus from facing his joy stealers head on. Joy stealers look out, Jesus is heading your way! We must face our problems the same way or the joy stealers will continue to keep us frozen in place joyless and directionless.

> Finally, he said to his disciples, "Let's go back to Judea".
> But his disciples objected. "Rabbi," they said, "only a few
> days ago the people in Judea were trying to stone you.
> Are you going there again?" (John 11:8)

Jesus even knowing what lies ahead for him in Judea, leads the disciples there. We need to face our situations the same way as Jesus faced those Joy Stealers, head on full speed forward.

The disciples, somewhat like you and me perhaps, try to dissuade Jesus from going, "Are you going there again?" I am sure they did not want to say anything stronger to Jesus. But their message to Him was clear. But Jesus's message was clear also. Face those joy stealers head on and send them running.

Then he said, our friend Lazarus has fallen asleep, but now I will go and wake him up. The disciples said, "Lord, if he is sleeping, he will soon get better! They thought Jesus meant Lazarus was simply sleeping, but Jesus meant Lazarus had died. So he told them plainly, "Lazarus is dead. And for your sakes, I'm glad I wasn't there for now you will really believe. Come let's go see him." Thomas, nicknamed the Twin said to his fellow disciples, "Let's go too-and die with Jesus." (John 11:11–16)

In these verses in the Gospel of John, Jesus tells the disciples why he is going to Judea. Lazarus has died. In verse 15 Jesus tells them that he is glad he was not there for Lazarus because now the disciples will really believe. I am not sure that statement really sunk in to the disciples because of Thomas's comment about what was going to happen when they went to Judea. Sure, Jesus we will go with you to Judea, go to Judea and die with you there. I think Thomas, and maybe some of the other disciples, were very uncomfortable going to Judea. He was uncomfortable and maybe a little fearful. These emotions were blocking Thomas's ability to hear what Jesus was saying. We all have that same problem. When we are facing fear, depression, loneliness, pain, anxiety, panic attacks, or any other condition, they block our ability to hear and understand God's word. Try as we might it is very hard to concentrate and to hear what God says. Often at this point all we hear is ourselves. The joy stealers have snuck in and taken over. The solution is to turn to Jesus as our example and face those joy stealers head on. Kick those joy stealers out. One at a time, one step at a time. Verse 7 tells us Jesus said, "Let's go back to Judea." As he faced those joy stealers in Judea it took Jesus one step at a time, just the same as us. Jesus is our example as we take one step forward just as he was the disciple's example. The disciple's certainly seemed to be feeling fear as they faced the journey to Judea. As Jesus lead them one step at a time he showed them how to face their joy stealers. And as we take one step forward those joy stealers will take a step backward until those joy stealers are gone for good.

As I was studying on this scripture towards the end of Jesus's ministry, it brought to mind another scripture at the beginning of Jesus's ministry, where Jesus faces the joy stealers head on also.

> The next day there was a wedding celebration in the village of Cana in Galilee. Jesus's mother was there, and Jesus and his disciples were also invited to the celebration. The wine supply ran out during the festivities, so Jesus's mother told him, "They have no more wine." Dear woman, "that's not our problem." Jesus replied. "My time has not yet come." But his mother told the servants, "Do whatever he tells you." (John 2:1–5)

It is interesting to me that when the supply of wine ran out Jesus's mother was aware of this. It makes me wonder if she was involved in the wedding ceremony somehow. One thing it shows us about Jesus's mother is that she was compassionate. She did not want the bride and groom or the groom's family to be embarrassed because there was no more wine. Once the news that the wine was gone started spreading, the joy stealers were the ones who were going to be having a party. Joy stealers just love spreading bad embarrassing news. Jesus's mother comes to him and tells him, "They have no more wine." Another thing it shows us about Jesus's mother is that she is comfortable bringing problems to Jesus. At this point in Jesus's ministry he has performed no miracles, according to scripture. Yet his mother comes and brings the, "they ran out of wine", problem to him. I can just hear my grandchildren saying, "yes, so?" but of course my grandchildren are not the Messiah.

> "Dear woman, that's not our problem." Jesus replied.
> "My time has not yet come." (John 2:4)

Jesus answers his mother that the wine running out was not his problem. And then perhaps to soften his answer he explains why it is not his problem and that is because his time has not yet come. His ministry on earth has not yet begun, I wonder as he is answering her if he is thinking ahead to when he is ministering to the people of Judea, healing the sick and casting out demons. Thinking of the time when there are so many people coming to see him that he and his disciples did not even have time to eat (Mark 6:31). For Jesus taking time now to enjoy a simple village festival; a wedding, with his family and friends, before he began his pubic ministry may have been a wonderful joyful experience.

I believe for many of us today, when we have a very busy time coming up on our schedule, we will often take a brief vacation or time away beforehand if possible. It helps to clear our minds and lower our stress level and put joy in our heart before our "busy time" arrives, if we let God minister to us. I know for myself, once I have done this I am now ready to tackle whatever is on my schedule. Also, by doing this we keep the joy stealers away. They have no opening to sneak in when we are keeping joy in our hearts. It seems when we do not take the time to "take a breath" before our busy time, we start out in a state of stress and low level depression. That is not a good way to begin a time when you have a very full plate and no time for rest. Starting a time of busyness in an emotional state such as this is starting with one strike against you. Doing this leaves openings for the joy stealers to come in and not only steal any joy you have but to begin telling you all the lies they love to tell. The joy stealers tell you that you are a failure, you will never accomplish your goal. They tell you that no one loves you, that you will always feel this way. These are just a few of the lies the joy stealers love to tell. Do not believe them. They will do and say anything to keep the joy from your heart.

> Guard your heart above all else, for it determines the
> course of your life. (Proverbs 4:23)

This Scripture from Proverbs is wise counsel. We must guard our heart and the joy that is in it, for if we keep our joy the course of our life will be joy-filled. As we are attempting to fight off the joy stealers it will be difficult because we started off in a difficult emotional state. The first step is to remember what the Lord has done for you. As the joy stealers are attacking you with their lies, just remember one thing Jesus has done for you. This will remind those joy stealers that you belong to Jesus Christ. The second step is to remember a Joy blessing, something that brings you joy, Praise the Lord! The third step is to remember your favorite scripture. Remember it and repeat it and watch those joy stealers turn tail and run away. The fourth step is friends. Find a friend to bring you up, not down. The fifth step brings us back to Jesus's mother. When she had a problem she turned to Jesus. That is always what we should do. Turn to Jesus. He will send those joy stealers running. These are just a few of the steps to take to send those joy stealers running. They are in no particular order. Use them and the joy stealers will be sent away, And joy will reign in your heart.

> But his mother told the servants, "Do whatever he tells you". (John 2:5)

After Jesus's mother told him that the wine had run out Jesus replied first that it was not their problem, then second that his time had not yet come. Now, like any good mother, Jesus's mother totally ignored what Jesus said, and proceeded as if she knew her son Jesus was going to do what she was asking. I believe this tells us something about the relationship between Jesus and his mother. It must have been a close relationship for his mother to expect him to do what she asked even though he had responded negatively to her request. The fact that Joseph is not mentioned at all in these scripture verses may be an indication that he had died. If that was the case, that made Jesus the head of the household. In those days the head of the household was in charge. His word was the law. For Jesus's mother to expect Jesus, the head of the household to do what she wanted was very unusual. I believe this shows us that Jesus and his mother shared a very special bond, a bond that did not care about rules and rituals.

We can look to this special bond Jesus had with his mother and understand that when we ask Jesus into our heart we also will have that special bond with Jesus. A bond that does not care about rules and rituals. A bond that is so close that even when Jesus, for whatever reason, may at first respond negatively to our request there is hope that as he responded favorably to his mother's request he also will respond favorably to our request.

> Standing nearby were six stone water jars, used for Jewish ceremonial washing. Each could hold twenty to thirty gallons. Jesus told the servants, "Fill the jars with

water." When the jars had been filled, he said, "Now
dip some out, and take it to the master of ceremonies."
So the servants followed his instructions. (John 2:6–8)

Jesus's mother told the servants to do whatever Jesus told them to
do. I can just imagine the servants looking from his mother to Jesus,
thinking, "huh, now what?" But I do not think Jesus left them wondering
very long. Jesus told the servants to fill the jars used for ceremonial
washing with water. These jars were used for foot washing and hand
washing. Jews became ceremonial defiled (unclean) during the normal
circumstances of daily life and were cleansed by pouring water over their
hands as described by Jewish law. I am thinking the servants thought, ok
we will be drinking water for the rest of the night! The water jugs held
up to 30 gallons each. They were filled to the brim with water turned
to wine. That would make about 90 bottles of wine. When Jesus turns
water to wine he does it abundantly! The best wine and more and more
of it. There were a couple of things the servants did not know. These
are not just ordinary jars used for ceremonial washing. These jars are
holy, set aside for God's service. And it was not just anyone directing
the filling of the jars. It was Jesus, our Lord and Savior. Jesus took those
jars, used for ceremonial washing, and said now the jars will be used for
a new purpose, they are still holy and set apart for the service of God.
Now instead of being used for ceremonial washing these jars will be used
first to turn water into the best wine. Second these jars will be used to
save the grooms family from the embarrassment of running out of wine.
Third, these jars will be used to bring Glory to Jesus as he performs his
first miracle and begins his public ministry.

If jars could rejoice I believe these jars would be dancing! These
jars went from being ordinary ceremonial jars, to jars used by Jesus
for amazing purposes. We are like those jars. We start out as ordinary
people doing ordinary things and then we meet Jesus Christ up close
and personal and ask Jesus to come and live in our heart and we are no
longer the ordinary person we were. We meet the extra ordinary God
and he changes us ordinary people into people who with his help are
used for amazing purposes.

When the master of ceremonies tasted the water that was now wine, not knowing where it had come from (though, of course, the servants knew), he called the bridegroom over. "A host always serves the best wine first," he said. "Then, when everyone has had a lot to drink, he brings out the less expensive wine. But you have kept the best until now!" (John 2:9–10)

Jesus told the servants in verse 8 to, 'dip some out', and take it to the master of ceremonies. So the servants followed his instructions and took some to the master of ceremonies. I wonder what was going through this person, the master of ceremonies, thoughts at this point. I wonder if this person knew they had run out of wine. If the master of ceremonies knew they had run out of wine, I wonder if he was prepared for some really poor quality wine and was so surprised when he tasted God powered wine. I know only a very small amount of how he felt.

Many years ago a friend and I were putting on a banquet. Between the two of us somehow we managed to advertise that we would have homemade pie for desert. My friend and I set a date, the day before the banquet to make and bake the pies. I remember mentioning to my husband that I was surprised that my friend was such a good pie maker that she was up to making that many pies, because I knew nothing about making a pie. I arrived that next morning and we got our pie making supplies out and we stood there looking at each other. My friend said, ok, go ahead, and start making the pies. I said, "What!" Neither one of us could make a pie if our life depended on it. Much laughter commenced and a very large amount of prayer. In the middle of our laughter a miracle walked through the door. Two of our friends walked in and asked what we were doing. We stopped laughing long enough to answer, "Making pies". They answered, "No you aren't, and, that is not how you make a pie." Which I am sorry to tell you, at that point, just made us laugh harder. Those two wonderful ladies gently took over the kitchen and in no time at all they had produced all the pies needed for the banquet. God sent them that day to make, "Miracle pies." Without them, there would have been no pies that day. The next day at the banquet everyone proclaimed they had never tasted such good pie. Two women who said yes to God, and simple ingredients blessed by God, turned into a simple miracle that day. We acknowledged God's Glory and praised Him for saving my friend and me the embarrassment of serving store bought cookies for desert at the banquet. We have never forgotten the, "miracle of the pies". We praise His Name and thank Him for His loving kindness.

At the wedding in Cana, after the Master of Ceremonies tasted the wine he called the bridegroom over. Now, I really wonder what the bridegroom is thinking. I believe he knows they have run out of wine. Does he wonder what the master of ceremonies is going to say to him? Is he thinking about how he is going to explain running out of wine? The master of ceremonies tells him, "a host always serves the best wine first, but you have kept the best until now!" (John 2:10) This wine, water turned into wine by the power of Jesus Christ, was the best wine. When Jesus is involved there is nothing better!

> This miraculous sign at Cana in Galilee was the first time Jesus revealed his glory. And his disciples believed in him. (John 2:11)

This miraculous sign was the first time Jesus revealed his glory. Jesus had not before this publicly performed any signs, wonders, or healings. As his disciples witnessed this miracle they believed in him. Our faith deepens as we experience Jesus working in our life and in the lives of our friends and family. As our faith deepens our joy increases until our joy knows no bounds and fills our hearts. Our hearts become so full of joy there is no room for the joy stealers.

In our Scripture from the gospel of John 11:14–16 we learned that the joy stealers come in and block our ability to hear and understand God's word. We then must turn to Jesus as our example and face those joy stealers head on. We will kick those joy stealers out as we draw closer to Jesus. Just as Jesus's mother turned to Jesus when the joy stealers came to the wedding in Cana with the intent of not only stealing joy but causing embarrassment and gossip. Jesus's mother turned to Jesus and as she did Jesus began to take charge and as he did the joy stealers faded away.

THOUGHTS ON LIVING JOYFULLY:

Do you feel God has to work to get your attention or do you believe you are very good at listening for God's voice?

How would you rate your prayer life? Poor, Good, Very Good, Excellent. Why?

Jesus faces his difficult situations head on. Are you like Jesus, moving full speed ahead to face your difficult situation? Or do you try to avoid your difficult situation? Jesus faced his joy stealers head on and sent them running. Meditate on ways you can face your joy stealers.

Contemplate why Jesus told his Mother, "That is not our problem. Jesus replied. My time has not yet come." John 2:4

Do you take time for yourself before a busy time on your calendar? Why or why not?

Proverbs 4:23 – Guard your heart above all else. Do not let your joy out! Which of the five steps works the best for you to keep the joy stealers away and the joy in your heart?

Do you come to the Throne of Grace with a prayer request humbly and meekly or boldly and confidently? Explain.

John 2:6–8 As Jesus proceeds to do as requested by his Mother, consider the thoughts and emotions of the people affected, (Master of Ceremonies, The Servants, Disciples, Groom) who do you think is most astonished by the Miracle? Why?

The author tells of a time of making, "Miracle Pies". Has anything like this ever happened in your experience? Explain

Prayerfully consider in the last year how your ability to let Jesus be in charge has progressed. On a scale of 1 to 10 with 10 being the best you could do, how would you rate your self today?

CHAPTER TEN

No bucket needed

When I was young my family and my extended family bought property on a river several hours north of where we lived. Each family bought a lot on the river to camp on. One of the first things my father wanted to do on his property was to put down a well and get water on his property. So he proceeded to set up a pipe system that went into the ground that he and others would hit with another pipe to pound it further into the ground until my father hit water. This vacation spot on the river was a wonderful place to grow up and then for my kids to spend time at. The only real draw back was the fact that my father was having trouble hitting water. And that was certainly not for lack of trying. The vacation spots on the river were used a lot by my family and my extended family. We loved spending time with my aunts and uncles and cousins. The time when everyone gathered together was on holidays. On holidays you could count on many family and friends coming to camp and enjoying the fellowship together. This also meant my father and other family members who were gathered there would bang on the pipe going down seeking water. This process went on for years. It was like a family hobby. Come to the family vacation property and bang on the pipe looking for water. I am not talking about just working on this well a couple of weekends a year. We used this vacation property almost every weekend.

Working on the well was a continuous process. For year after year after year. Until the amazing thing happened. My dad hit water. Not a lot of water. The reward for all that hard work was so sweet because God provided just what we needed.

Over the course of all those years, working on that well, an inch at a time, I am sure the joy stealers were doing their best to steal my dad's joy about having a well on his property. The joy stealers were doing their best to steal my dad's joy about how great he felt about his vacation property. But through all the years he was banging on the pipe trying to hit water, he never lost his joy. God blessed my dad, when he hit water, he did not have a very large flow, but the flow did not stop! My dad hit a flowing well. Once the water started it just kept on flowing. When we are faithful, even when we are not seeing results of our labor, God will honor us with blessings that never cease.

> The faithful love of the LORD never ends! His mercies never cease. Great is his faithfulness; his mercies begin afresh each morning. (Lamentations 3:22–23)

As we are faithful those joy stealers will cease to bother us.

> So he left Judea and returned to Galilee. He had to go through Samaria on the way. Eventually he came to the Samaritan village of Sychar, near the field that Jacob gave to his son Joseph. Jacob's well was there; and Jesus, tired from the long walk, sat wearily beside the well about noontime. (John 4:3–6)

Jesus, in order to avoid conflict, left Judea and returned to Galilee. The quickest, shortest route was through Samaria. Most Jews avoided this route and took the longer route, by first going east to Jericho, then following the Jordan Valley north. We find Jesus taking the shorter route, through Samaria, perhaps because he had a divine appointment with someone. Jesus came to the Samaritan Village of Sychar tired from his long walk he sat down beside Jacob's well about noon. It is interesting that Jesus is by himself as he is resting by the well. It is not often that we find Jesus alone, without any of his followers with him. I believe this also was by design – heavenly design. Jesus has a divine appointment and he has sent his followers off on an errand so he could make his divine appointment. That is where we find Jesus now. Tired and weary, waiting beside the well. No matter how tired and weary Jesus is, he always has time for us, he will always wait for us. What a wonderful, joyful blessing!

> Soon a Samaritan woman came to draw water, and Jesus said to her, "Please give me a drink." He was alone at the time because his disciples had gone into the village to buy some food. The woman was surprised, for Jews refuse to have anything to do with Samaritans. She said to Jesus, "You are a Jew, and I am a Samaritan woman. Why are you asking me for a drink?" (John 4:7–9)

As the Samaritan woman comes to the well that day she had a divine appointment with Jesus. She did not know she had this appointment, it was not marked on her calendar, and no one called her on her cell phone to remind her of her appointment. Never the less Jesus was waiting for her. This appointment was made by divine hands. Some days are like that, they start out as ordinary days and turn into days divine hands had appointed for us to hear an important message from God. Ordinary days turned into extraordinary days by our awesome God. Just like the Samaritan woman we never know what the Lord has in store for us, we just need to be open to His word and His leading. To go where he wants us to go and to do what he wants us to do.

The Samaritan woman is coming to Jacob's well to draw water. Verse 6 tells us that it is about noontime, a very unusual time for women to come to the well to draw water. It was normal for the women to come in the cool of the day to draw water, either in the early morning or the evening. The women came together not only to collect the water but also so they could talk and share the news of the village with each other. Remember these women did not have newspaper, television, cellphones, Facebook, twitter, or whatever means of communication we have today! They relied on word of mouth and gathering together was their main means of sharing the news of their households and family. These women looked forward to their time together and chatted joyfully on the way to the well and back to their homes. Our Samaritan woman came at noontime apparently to avoid the other women of the village. She is an outcast and perhaps has felt the stares of the other women and of course has heard the words of gossip that has been said about her. As she comes to the well at noon she is trying to avoid the situation that drains her joy.

As the Samaritan woman is coming to the well, I wonder if when she noticed "a man" sitting beside the well, from a ways off, her feet began to hesitate. Did her steps begin to slow? Did she question in her mind, "Why was a 'man', at the well at the time she wanted to draw water?" Did she quietly grumble because she came at this time to avoid people who would criticize her and now here was a man, sitting where she wanted to draw from the well? As she drew closer to the well the man became clearer to her. As she arrived at the well, Jesus tired and weary from his travels asked her for a drink. Vs 7. Soon a Samaritan woman came to draw water, and Jesus said to her, "Please give me a drink." Here is the divine appointment. Jesus, alone, tired, asks the Samaritan woman for a drink of water. And the Samaritan woman looks at Jesus and, what?

The thing about divine appointments is that we are often surprised by them. They may come while we least expect them. We are not always prepared for the divine appointments God has for us. Did you ever have a nagging feeling that you were forgetting to do something? Maybe you were! Next time, stop and pray and ask God if there was something He wanted you to do today. Maybe God had an important task for you to accomplish. We never want to miss an opportunity to keep a divine appointment with God.

The Samaritan woman finds herself surprised. The man, the Jew, at the well asks her a question. She was prepared to be ignored by him. Perhaps with a look of contempt thrown her way, the man was a Jew after all, and she was a Samaritan. As she was attempting to quietly slip by him, he stops her with his question. Perhaps with a bit of confusion she asks, "Why are you asking me for a drink? You are a Jew and I am a Samaritan woman." Vs. 9. If I was her I would have been thinking hey, don't you know Jews and Samaritans do not talk to each other!

Jesus replied, "If you only knew the gift God has for you and who you are speaking to, you would ask me, and I would give you living water." But sir, you don't have a rope or a bucket," she said," and this well is very deep. Where would you get this living water? And besides, do you think you're greater than our ancestor Jacob, who gave us this well? How can you offer better water than he and his sons and his animals enjoyed?" Jesus replied, "Anyone who drinks this water will soon become thirsty again. But those who drink the water I give will never be thirsty again. It becomes a fresh bubbling spring within them, giving them eternal life." "Please sir," the woman said, "give me this water! Then I'll never be thirsty again, and I won't have to come here to get water." (John 4:10–15)

In verse 10 Jesus replied to her, "if you only knew the gift God has for you and who you are speaking to, you would ask me, and I would give you living water." The Samaritan woman very much wants this living water. In Jewish Culture "dead water" referred to standing and stored water. 'Living Water' was water that moved, water from rivers, springs, and rainfall. They considered this moving water as coming directly from God. I love this thought, as I consider John baptizing in the Jordan River.

Then Jesus went from Galilee to the Jordan River to be baptized by John. But John tried to talk him out of it. "I am the one who needs to be baptized by you," he said, "so why are you coming to me?" But Jesus said, "It should be done, for we must carry out all that God requires." So John agreed to baptize him. After his baptism, as Jesus came up out of the water, the heavens were opened and he saw the Spirit of God descending like a dove and settling on him. And a voice from heaven said, "This is my dearly loved Son, who brings me great joy." (Matthew 3:13–17)

Verse 17 are wonderful words, words I think all of us long to hear God say about us: This is my dearly loved Son, who brings me great joy. No joy stealer will ever be able to take away the joy we feel from bringing joy to God.

Our Samaritan woman is very interested in the Living Water Jesus is offering. In verse 11 she points out that the well is very deep and Jesus does not have a rope or a bucket. Then she says where would you get this Living Water? Our Samaritan woman is very observant, she looks around and sees no rope or bucket. She also sees no Living Water. I wonder what she is beginning to think of Jesus. Then she seems to come to a decision about Jesus, and asks in verse 12, "And besides, do you think you're greater than our ancestor Jacob, who gave us this well? How can you offer better water than he and his sons and his animals enjoyed?" When I read this verse it just makes me laugh. It reminds me of kids on a playground saying, "Oh, yeah, my brother is stronger than your brother." I think every time our Samaritan woman begins to get confused she asks Jesus questions, such as, "How can you offer better water?" Jesus replied, "Anyone who drinks this water will soon become thirsty again. But those who drink the water I give will never be thirsty again. It becomes a fresh, bubbling spring within them, giving them eternal life." Vs 13-14. When my dad was working so hard trying to put in a well on his vacation place, he finally hit water, water that kept on flowing. That flowing well brought joy and refreshment to my father and all that came to drink from the well. But this well lacked one thing that Jesus's water has. Anyone who drinks the water Jesus gives will never be thirsty again and they will have Eternal Life! Jesus's water is enriched with the Holy Spirit. Jesus plus the Holy Spirt equals life giving water that brings eternal life.

The Samaritan woman jumps right on this, she sees the benefit of this water. The earthly benefit of this water; she will not have to come here to get water anymore. She will not have to endure the stares and the rumors. This water will set her free from all her problems with the other women in the village. Of course she wants this wonderful water.

"Go and get your husband," Jesus told her. "I don't have a husband," the woman replied. Jesus said, "You're right! You don't have a husband—for you have had five husbands, and you aren't even married to the man you're living with now. You certainly spoke the truth!" "Sir," the woman said, "you must be a prophet. So tell me, why is it that you Jews insist that Jerusalem is the only place of worship, while we Samaritans claim it is here at Mount Gerizim, where our ancestors worshiped?" Jesus replied, "Believe me, dear woman, the time is coming when it will no longer matter whether you worship the Father on this mountain or in Jerusalem. You Samaritans know very little about the one you worship, while we Jews know all about him, for salvation comes through the Jews. But the time is coming – indeed it's here now – when true worshipers will worship the Father in spirit and truth. The Father is looking for those who will worship him that way. For God is Spirit, so those who worship him must worship in spirit and in truth." The woman said, "I know the Messiah is coming – the one who is called Christ. When he comes, he will explain everything to us." Then Jesus told her, "I AM the Messiah!" (John 4:16–26)

Jesus catches right on to the fact that she has missed the main point. To help guide her in the right direction Jesus asks her to go and get her husband. The Samaritan woman tells Jesus she does not have a husband. Jesus replies with a brief history of her marriages, ending with the fact that she is not married to the man she is living with now, and tells her that she has spoken the truth.

As we have seen when the Samaritan woman is confused or conflicted she asks Jesus a question. In verse 19 she declares that Jesus must be a prophet. That begins a discussion with Jesus about worship. In verse 23 Jesus tells her that true worshippers worship the Father in Spirit and in truth. The Samaritan woman responds with, "I know the Messiah is coming." Then Jesus told her, "I AM the Messiah!" Now I do not know about the Samaritan woman, or about you, but this scripture still rocks my socks off! The Samaritan woman says one day the Messiah is coming, and Jesus says, hey, open your eyes He is standing right in front of you! How often do each of us need to be reminded that Jesus is right beside us?

> And be sure of this: I am with you always, even to the end of the age. (Matthew 28:20b)

> Just then his disciples came back. They were shocked to find him talking to a woman, but none of them had the nerve to ask, "What do you want with her?" or "Why are you talking to her?" The woman left her water jar beside the well and ran back to the village, telling everyone, "Come and see a man who told me everything I ever did! Could he possibly be the Messiah?" So the people came streaming from the village to see him. (John 4:27–30)

Just then then the disciples came back. Considering the situation between the Jews and the Samaritans and the social customs of a woman not talking to a man who is not her husband, the disciples were surprised to see Jesus talking to the Samaritan woman. Yet none of them had the courage to ask Jesus about him going against those customs. When the disciples returned the Samaritan woman left her water jug beside the well and ran to tell everyone in the village, "Come and see a man who told me everything I ever did! Could he possibly be the Messiah?" I see this with a smile on my face, this Samaritan woman who so wanted to stay away from the village people that she came in the very heat of the day to draw water at the well, here she is now, after meeting Jesus, running – (yes running) to the village so she could tell everyone about Jesus. I so wish I could remember the time I was so excited to tell someone about Jesus that I ran, (yes, ran) to tell them the Good News. Right now as I write this I am envious of the Samaritan Woman. She had the desire to share Jesus and the excitement and energy to match. I pray that God will ignite that Spirit of desire and excitement to share Jesus with others within me and within those reading these words. May we run to share Jesus with those around us. As the Samaritan woman tells the village people about Jesus, verse 29 tells us she says, "Come and see a man who told me everything I ever did!" I wonder if when she said that, in her mind she added, 'and he loves me anyway!' I wonder if every time she retold this story she started saying it under her breath a little in awe, 'and Jesus loves me anyway!!' I feel that way sometimes. I should feel that way every day! He loves me. I am astonished! I go up for communion, humbly, knowing I am not worthy. But like the Samaritan woman, he loves me anyway. Thank you Lord Jesus, for loving me.

The Samaritan woman was so convincing in her telling about Jesus that verse 30 tells us:

So the people came streaming from the Village to see Him.

In my mind I see everyone she talked to dropping what they were doing and going to see Jesus. Of course I do not know if that is true, I just see it that way in my mind. How do you see it?

As the Samaritan woman is telling the village people about Jesus, Jesus is talking to the disciples about food. Food? Yup, food.

> Then Jesus explained: My nourishment comes from doing the will of God, who sent me, and from finishing His work. You know the saying, "four months between planting and harvest". But I say, wake up and look around. The fields are already ripe for harvest. The harvesters are paid good wages, and the fruit they harvest is people brought to eternal life. What joy awaits both the planter and the harvester alike! (John 4:34–36)

In these verses Jesus is talking to the disciples. If you look at verse 35 and imagine as Jesus says wake up and look around, the disciples doing as Jesus says, and lift up their heads and look around and at that very moment the people from the village streaming to see Jesus come into view. The disciples with their mouths open hear Jesus say, "The fields are already ripe for harvest".

That, my friend, will make an impact on you. That, my friend, will knock your socks off. Jesus has a way of getting through to us in a mighty way. The fields are ripe for the harvest. The harvest is people brought to eternal life. That is Joy to our very soul. A church near where

I live had a purpose/mission statement that made a very big impact on me. Their Purpose Statement was:

"Save the Lost at any Cost
'Cuz People live Forever."

A mission statement is the overall goal or purpose of the organization or Church. Perhaps being Christians our goal may be to spread the Gospel. Or to Save the Lost at any Cost.

Many Samaritans from the village believed in Jesus because the woman had said, "He told me everything I ever did!" When they came out to see him, they begged him to stay in their village. So he stayed for two days, long enough for many more to hear his message and believe. Then they said to the woman, "Now we believe, not just because of what you told us, but because we have heard him ourselves. Now we know that he is indeed the Savior of the world." (John 4:39–42)

The Samaritan woman witnessed to the people of the village all about Jesus. Because of what she said they were excited to meet Jesus and hear his message. Verse 42 tells us that now they believed because they heard Jesus themselves, not just because of what the Samaritan woman had told them. As a Christian we can lead others to Jesus by our words and by our actions, but it is the saving Grace of Jesus Christ that gives eternal life.

> For God loved the world so much that he gave his one and only Son, so that everyone who believes in him will not perish but have eternal life. (John 3:16)

> So just as sin ruled over all people and brought them to death, now God's wonderful grace rules instead, giving us right standing with God and resulting in eternal life through Jesus Christ our Lord. (Romans 5:21)

The people of the village said to the Samaritan woman we believe because we have heard him ourselves. There are times when we come from a long line of Christians, family with strong faith. They, like the Samaritan woman, can tell us about Jesus, they can tell us about their faith, but that is what it is, "their faith". Their faith will save them but it will not save anyone else. Being a Christian is a personal faith. Others faith walk will draw us to Jesus and to reading the Bible and to us saying Yes, Lord I believe in You. I repent or put away my sins and give my life to you. And like the people of the Samaritan village we can say Lord Jesus we know you are indeed the Savior of the World. Then your heart is filled with joy!

THOUGHTS ON LIVING JOYFULLY:

The author relates a story about her family's vacation property and her father's desire to put a well on the property. The author states that it became a family hobby to, "bang on the pipe", trying to put down the pipe seeking water. Many years and much trying occurred before water was found. Can you relate to the faithfulness of those seeking the water? Can you imagine the joy that was felt when water began to flow?

Lamentations 3:22-23 These verses tell us God's mercies begin afresh each morning. What do these verses mean to you?

John 4:3–6 As you read these verses and realize that Jesus is at Jacob's well waiting for the Samaritan woman do you also know that he will wait for you? How does that knowledge make you feel? How does that knowledge affect your life?

Have you ever felt like the outcast? Avoiding everyone in order to keep your joy? How has Jesus helped return you to your rightful place in your "village"?

Have you ever had a "quiet place" that you would be reluctant to share with someone? How would you feel to see someone there as you came near it? What action would you take?

When we try to hide something from God we soon are reminded that God knows all. Have you ever done this? How did you feel when you realized, like the Samaritan woman, that God is all knowing?

When you read the words Jesus spoke, "I Am the Messiah!" How do those words impact you? Have they become "old hat", to you? Just more words in the bible? Or do they, like the author, knock your socks off!

How do you feel when you realize that Jesus "loves you anyway"? Close your eyes and whisper, Jesus loves me anyway. Jesus, Loves me, no matter what. Now do that 10 times a day for the next week. After that week answer the question again.

Do you have a family with a strong faith? Their faith will lead us to Jesus, but we must make our own decision for Jesus Christ. Have you asked Jesus in your heart? If not, pray about the love and grace of Jesus Christ. Jesus is waiting for you.

CHAPTER ELEVEN

God of last chances

In the last chapter after the Samaritan woman talked to Jesus and learned he was the Messiah, she dropped everything, (in her case it was the bucket she used to draw water), and ran back to the village to tell everyone her good news.

> The woman left her water jar beside the well and ran back to the village, telling everyone, "Come and see a man who told me everything I ever did, could he possibly be the Messiah?" (John 4:28–29)

When we have good news it is normal to not be able to wait to tell everyone about it. Sharing good news is a natural desire. In Jesus's last appearance on earth he had a message for the disciples. As they gathered, he talked with them.

> Jesus came and told his disciples, "I have been given all authority in heaven and on earth. Therefore, go and make disciples of all the nations, baptizing them in the name of the Father and the Son and the Holy Spirit. Teach these new disciples to obey all the commands

I have given you. And be sure of this: I am with you
always, even to the end of the age. (Matthew 28:18–20)

The disciples are on the mountain waiting for Jesus. As Jesus taught
them and gave them his final earthly instructions he then ascended into
Heaven. His message to his disciples, then and now, is very powerful.
To go and make disciples. To Go. We cannot stay on the mountain top.
Waiting for people to come to us. We love it on the mountain top, it is a
wonderful place to be. The mountain top is a place of victory. It can be
a place where we meet Jesus face to face as with the disciples and Jesus.
So we love the mountain top. But there are not very many people up
there on that mountain top. We have to leave that place and, "Go". Go
where? Everywhere – make disciples of all the nations. Go where you
live, shop, worship, vacation, visit for entertainment, etc. We live in a
bubble sometimes, a little Christian bubble, thinking everyone around us
is a Christian. No need to speak the Good News to the lady at the store
because she knows Jesus. Really? Maybe? Have you talked to her about
Jesus? Have I? Maybe her faith is failing, maybe she needs a faith boost
today. Maybe she needed you or me and our words of encouragement of
how faithful our Lord and Savior Jesus Christ is. We need to break out of
our bubble and see how much the people of the world need Jesus. How
much the people of your town or village need Jesus. Wherever you are,
go and make disciples. Use your words, your actions and your smiles.
Joy is contagious. For the people you meet, you may be the only one
who smiled at them. I heard "You may be the only Bible some people
read today"-by William J Toms.

Imitate God, therefore, in everything you do, because
you are his dear children. (Ephesians 5:1)

This scripture reminds me of a young child following in his father's
footsteps. Happy to be spending time with his daddy, he is intent on
doing everything exactly like his daddy. This image makes me smile
every time it comes to my mind. When my son was very young, my
parents were remodeling their house. My son and my father had a very
close relationship, and when we came to visit my son would "help" my

father in his construction on the new bathroom he was building for my mother. I remember this construction project very well, as if it were yesterday, instead of over 35 years ago. My father would pick up his hammer and my son would pick up his toy hammer. Whatever my father did my son would try to do also. He loved his grandfather so much that he wanted to do and be just like him.

Our scripture from Ephesians says, "Imitate God, therefore, in everything you do, because you are his dear children." My son was doing this for my dad, at his very young age he idolized my father. This connection between my son and my father was very strong and remained so as my son, young as he was, grew in his faith. Attending church on Sunday morning was a part of the week he looked forward to. His friends also attended the same church and they were all in Sunday school together.

After Sunday Worship my family would travel to my parent's home for Sunday dinner. This is how we spent most Sundays when my children were young. Sunday school, worship, and then Sunday dinner at my parent's home. (It was not always easy to get us and the kids out of the house with smiles on our faces and joy in our hearts!) My parents loved my kids, and my kids loved my parents. It was a wonderful way to spend our Sunday afternoon. My daughter and my mom had a wonderful loving relationship. As soon as we arrived I would be busy in the kitchen helping and talking with my mom, and my daughter would be busy in my mom's closet. Looking for her prettiest high heeled shoes. My daughter could walk in those high heeled shoes better than I could! And by the way, she still can, she is a very, beautiful woman. Pretty soon in the kitchen my mom and I would hear clump, clump, clump coming from outside, and we would know that my daughter was outside walking in Grandma's high heeled shoes. Normally my mom would just smile, but on occasion she would cry out, my new shoes, and run out to substitute another pair for her granddaughter to walk in. My mom worked in the professional world and dressed up daily as she visited many offices in our area. I am not surprised my daughter is beautiful, I am sure it passed down to her from my mom. Then one afternoon as we were eating and talking my son spoke up, he looked at his grandfather and asked him, "What church do you go to Grandpa?" My parents were not attending church at that time. They had attended on and off throughout the years, but at that moment they were not going to church. At my son's question, it became very quiet at the table. My son was very serious in his question, and my father gave his question serious thought. He answered that they were not going to church right now, but that he thought it was a good time to go back to church. My son answered, "Good". My heart soared at that point and I thought of the scripture:

"And a little child will lead them all." (Isaiah 11:6)

We all think we cannot witness or lead another person to Christ, but even a little child, like my son, can witness and lead another person to Christ. My parents were in church the following week. The church they found was wonderful. My dad was baptized and made a public proclamation of faith in Jesus Christ. My mom and dad attended Bible Study together and they loved it. The Pastor taught the Bible Study and they became friends with him and his wife. All because of a young boy's words. My father died soon after those events happened. I cannot tell you how often I have thanked God that my son spoke up. I know he had the connection with my dad to allow his witness to be effective.

God has called all of us to, "Go and make disciples of all the nations." (Matthew 28:19a) Often it is family members we find most difficult to witness to. I do not know why that is, family are normally those closest to us and those we love. To me that means we want them in heaven with us. We ought to be able to talk to them about how wonderful heaven is and how to get there!

John 3:16 tells us:

> For God loved the world so much that he gave his one
> and only Son, so that everyone who believes in him will
> not perish but have eternal life.

This verse is a very good starting verse when witnessing. For one thing it is familiar to a lot of people. It is important to find a common ground you can build on before you begin witnessing in earnest. Also, always remember witnessing is built on prayer. When we begin witnessing prayer is necessary, because we rely on God to give us the words to say and we rely on the Holy Spirit to move in the person's life to ask Jesus in their heart. We are merely the instrument used to share the Gospel with the lost.

> One day Jesus called together his twelve disciples and gave them power and authority to cast out all demons and to heal all diseases. Then he sent them out to tell everyone about the Kingdom of God and to heal the sick. (Luke 9:1–2)

In Luke Chapter 9 Jesus gives his disciples the power and authority to cast out all demons and to heal all diseases. Then he sent them out to tell everyone about the Kingdom of God and to heal the sick. It is Jesus's desire that we go and tell everyone about the Kingdom of God. What a wonderful place the Kingdom of God is. In my mind the Kingdom of God is where God's people live in harmony and Joy in God's home and Jesus is the King and God is the BOSS! We should be shouting from the roof tops what a wonderful home God has for his people – The Kingdom of God.

> Early on Sunday morning, as the new day was dawning, Mary Magdalene and the other Mary went out to visit the tomb. Suddenly there was a great earthquake! For an angel of the Lord came down from heaven, rolled aside the stone, and sat on it. His face shone like lightning, and his clothing was as white as snow. The guards shook with fear when they saw him, and they fell into a dead faint. Then the angel spoke to the women "Don't be afraid!" he said. "I know you are looking for Jesus, who was crucified. He isn't here! He is risen from the dead, just as he said would happen. Come, see where his body was lying. And now, go quickly and tell his disciples that he was risen from the dead, and he is going ahead of you to Galilee. You will see him there. Remember what I have told you." The women ran quickly from the tomb.

> They were very frightened but also filled with great joy, and they rushed to give the disciples the angel's message. (Matthew 28:1–8)

After Jesus's Crucifixion Mary Magdalene and the other Mary went out to visit the tomb. They, like the disciples, were inside where they were staying, afraid of the Romans and the Jewish authorities. Yet these brave women set aside their fears and early in the morning they went out to visit Jesus's tomb. They are going to Jesus's tomb, not knowing what to expect. They are full of sorrow and fear. The future that they were so sure of just a few days ago has been shattered and the future they see now is very bleak. As they are walking to the tomb there is no joy between them. The joy stealers have done a good job of stealing all their joy.

I see Mary Magdalene and the other Mary as they are nearing the tomb, their steps become slower, their words become fewer, and more hushed. Then suddenly there is a great earthquake! Do the women clutch and hold on to each other? I think so, I know I would have! Now they are really frightened, for an angel of the Lord came down. (Angels in the New Testament are heavenly beings created by God to serve him and his creation. Angels are often messengers, they deliver messages from God to his people.) The guards, who were there guarding Jesus's tomb, shook with fear at the sight of the angel and fell into a dead faint. But the angel was very quick to speak to our very brave women and calm their fears, "Don't be afraid", the angel said. (Matthew 28:5) And went on to explain why they should not be afraid. In verse 6b the angel says, "Come, see where his body was lying." The angel of the Lord wanted the women to have the personal experience of seeing where Jesus's body was lying. Past tense. The angel wanted the women to see that Jesus's body was not there anymore. Wow, powerful stuff. The women must have been mouth open and eyes boggling. Well, ok, that is how I would have been. The first thing we need before we can go out and witness is personal experience. It is very hard to tell someone about something you have not experienced or done yourself. Once we have that personal experience we are then able to witness to others.

After the women had seen that Jesus was not there the angel said to them in verse 7: And now, go quickly and tell his disciples that he has risen from the dead, and he is going ahead of you to Galilee. You will see him there. Remember what I have told you.

After the women experienced seeing the empty tomb the angel tells them to go and tell. After our personal experience what are we to do but, go and tell. Our job is to go and tell. Meet Jesus, come and see Him, and then go and tell everyone! That is how the word is spread. I tell, and you tell and the world will know the wonderful Kingdom of God. There is a warning at the end of verse 7. The angel tells us: "Remember what I have told you." Why does the angel tell us this? The angel has just given us instructions on how to witness and spread the Gospel. Come and see and go and tell. One person tells one person who tells one person. The warning comes because this is God's plan for spreading the Gospel. How are you doing holding up your part of God's plan?

> The women ran quickly from the tomb. They were very
> frightened but also filled with great joy, and they rushed
> to give the disciples the angel's message. Verse 8

The women, frightened though they were, they were filled with great joy as they rushed to go and tell. They stepped out in faith to follow the angel's instructions. There are times when it takes courage to step out in faith. We know Jesus has our back, but still there is a residue of fear and it takes courage in the midst of our faith to step out of our comfort zone and follow God's plan. There is also great joy that fills our heart when we know we are following God's instructions.

My husband and I vacation several times a year in Mexico, (in fact I am typing this while I am sitting with a beautiful view of the Palm trees and the wonderful sunny sky). We have visited quite a few places in Mexico and we have enjoyed each place we have vacationed at. A few years ago God directed us to a beautiful location in Mexico. The people were so friendly there, we felt so welcomed. We take vacation trips for several reasons. One reason is probably the same as a lot of people, vacations are fun! When we are on vacation we do have fun, we swim and snorkel, and eat fresh fish, (which is somewhat hard to get where we live), and we take short walks, and enjoy our time in the sun. Another reason we take vacation trips is to renew our strength and energy. By that I mean mostly mine. With my illness I run out of both strength and energy very quickly. But there are those times that my husband needs his strength and energy renewed also. Returning to the warmth and sun and beautiful beaches we know so well, God is faithful and restores our strength and energy. We return home ready and able to do His work. Another byproduct of my illness is the inability to handle stress. As stress increases, the affect it has on my body increases also, which then causes me more stress, which then increases the affect it has on my body which then causes.........I do believe you understand my point. As I begin showing the effects of stress overload my husband and I know that a vacation is necessary in the near future. For me the effects of stress overload often are, (now, please realize my husband may have his own list of my stress behaviors!)Short temper, (what, me?), limited patience, speaking without thinking, and the biggest effect of stress overload is my pain threshold is vastly reduced, which increases the effect of all the other behaviors. For whatever reason God is able to finally break through my preoccupation and fog when I am on vacation.

The most amazing thing happens as God touches me and I feel His healing throughout my body, and I am filled with joy.

> The Lord is my strength and shield. I trust him with all
> my heart. He helps me, and my heart is filled with joy. I
> burst out in songs of thanksgiving. (Psalm 28:7)

I am filled with such joy. I have come and see. I have a personal experience of the Living Christ and I cannot wait to, "go and tell". My husband and I visit with a great number of people and it is our desire to share the Good News of Jesus Christ with everyone we meet. God has been so faithful and good to us. Directing our path and the people to us, often before we even get on the airplane. Nothing fills my heart with more joy than sharing Christ. Step out in faith and give it a try. God has your back and will be faithful to you as you begin sharing what he has done for you. As we return home, refreshed and renewed by our amazing God, we have been filled once again and are ready and able to resume the ministry God has called us to.

> Imitate God, therefore, in everything you do, because
> you are his dear children. (Ephesians 5:1)

The Apostle Paul tells us in Ephesians 5:1 that we are to imitate God in everything we do, because we are His dear children. Once we have asked Jesus into our heart and repented of our sins we become one of his Children. How do we imitate God? Jesus is our example. Jesus came and walked this earth to show us how to live. Everywhere Jesus went he told of God's Kingdom. Jesus preached and taught and healed everywhere he went, telling everyone about his Heavenly Father.

As we imitate Jesus and begin telling others about God's Kingdom our lives will be so filled with joy they will never be the same.

THOUGHTS ON LIVING JOYFULLY:

Matthew 28:18–20 the author says we need to break out of our bubble because the people of the world need Jesus. What is your experience with sharing the Gospel with others?

> Considering Matthew 28:19, how does this verse make
> you feel?

Ephesian 5:1 How are you at imitating God? As you prayerfully consider the next week how will you be more equipped to imitate God?

The author tells of her son helping lead his grandfather back to Christ. She says: We ought to be able to talk to people about how wonderful heaven is and how to get there! How is your witnessing going? Do you find it hard to witness to family? Why or why not?

Witness is built on Prayer. We rely on God to give us the words to say. Does this relieve you of some of the stress of witnessing? Why or why not?

The author describes her vision of the Kingdom of God. What is your vision of the Kingdom of God?

Matthew 28:1–8 Mary Magdalene and the other Mary went to the tomb even though they were full of sorrow and fear. At that point in the story, putting yourself in these women's shoes (or sandal's, as the case may be) would you be as brave as they were? What would your reaction have been to the earthquake and the appearance of the angel?

The author says: Our job is to go and tell. Meet Jesus, come and see Him and then, go and tell everyone! That is how the word is spread. I tell, and you tell and the world will know the wonderful Kingdom of God. How are you at keeping up your job of come and see and go and tell? Which part do you get stumbled up on?

Matthew 28:8 The women ran quickly from the tomb. They were very frightened, but also filled with great joy, and they rushed to give the disciples the angel's message. Here we see once again someone running to do God's will. Frightened, yes. But also filled with great joy and running to do as the angel commanded. When was the last time you ran with great joy to do God's will? When was the last time you ran to God?

CHAPTER TWELVE

Jesus loves me

Over the pages of this book I have given you a glimpse of my family as I was growing up. I was very close to both my parents. I had a wonderful childhood growing up with my brother. He was a great brother and taught me all the things I needed to know growing up, like how to go on a Snipe hunt, what wine to drink, and that the police cannot enter the house without a search warrant. We were great friends then and we are still great friends today.

My growing up years were stable as my family of four enjoyed time together camping and spending time with friends and family. My memories are full of love and laughter. I remember my first dance. My first dance was using my parent's dining room floor as the dance floor and my dad as the instructor. As I look back at that memory I cherish it. Around and around that dining room we went, my dad and I, at that moment in time I felt so grown up, and soon the dance lesson became more and more a dance and less and less a lesson, until it was just my dad and me dancing on that dance floor. I know in my heart that my dad is waiting for me in heaven and you can be sure there will be much dancing and rejoicing as we celebrate and worship our Heavenly Father.

As I married and had children my respect for my parents grew. Neither of my parents graduated from High School. When I was in Middle School they both took classes to get their Adult General Education Degrees. As I look back at all they had accomplished in their lives, without a formal education, I am amazed. There are many people today with much more education who have not accomplished nearly as much. My dad found a job working for our City Government and loved his job. My mother did not like working while my brother and I were in school, but life being what it was it became necessary for her to work and over the years she worked and was promoted and then took a consulting job in her area. All without a High School Diploma. My mother, Super mom, and Super worker. One Christmas as she was preparing the food for our family Christmas dinner she somehow broke her wrist. How this happened was a mystery. Off she went to the emergency room, x-rays, a cast, and pain pills. When she came home she was determined to not spoil our Christmas. Now we were teenagers at this point. Very capable of helping my dad put on the dinner. But that was not good enough for Super Mom. We did eventually get pills into her and off to bed she went. I think she woke up the day after Christmas! She was always there for us, love and joy and laughter. She always said she was powered by the sun, as she loved to sit in the sun and read her book. As her life was coming to an end we realized she was powered by the Son. What could be better? What could bring more joy?

The perfect time for the joy stealers to make an appearance. I am not certain when mom's dementia first began because mom was so good at hiding the signs of dementia. This woman who was so intelligent was slowly forgetting things. As much as she tried to hide all the signs and symptoms, those closest to her were able to perceive what was happening to her. This joy stealer brought me to my knees. This joy stealer got up in my face. This time as I got down on my knees crying and crying out to God, I remembered this Scripture:

> While knowledge makes us feel important, it is love that strengthens the church. Anyone who claims to know all the answers doesn't really know very much. But the person who loves God is the one whom God recognizes. (I Corinthians 8:1b–3)

God reminded me that He was not concerned about our knowledge, He was concerned about our love of Him. What relief flooded my soul, for I knew mom loved God. Relief and love sent those joy stealers away. But sadly that was not the only time I or my family was to be visited by the joy stealers. Dementia of any kind is a slow, cruel, disease. As mom's disease, (what name to put to it? Alzheimer's, diabetes related dementia?), progressed she had a harder time suppressing the signs of the disease. The day I went to her and sat down to discuss this with her was very difficult. She denied it at first, then told me it was none of my business. Then, for the first time ever, (though it would happen again and again), she kicked me out of her house. The joy stealer tried to enter in but I had come prayed up and powered up.

> Love never gives up, never loses faith, is always hopeful, and endures through every circumstance. (1 Corinthians 13:7)

No room for joy stealers! God, through much prayer, had helped me understand that it was the "disease", not mom who was in control. After much conversation with mom, I was able to get her to her doctor, which led to testing and medication, which did slow down her disease progression to some degree.

Amidst the sorrow there was joy. I loved to see mom smile. Those smiles were coming less frequently now. But, I knew they were there. If I could not see them, I knew God could. One thing that made her smile was her grandchildren and her great-grandchildren. Of course! She was a terrific mother. Also a terrific grandmother. Her great-granddaughter made a beautiful connection with mom. They loved each other so much. Hugs, sitting on Grandma's lap. It was so beautiful. We have a picture of mom sitting on the couch, full out laughing with her great-grandson sitting next to her laughing just as hard. It is a wonderful joyful picture. With this disease, like many others, you seek out and treasure your joy moments. No joy moment goes unnoticed. Some joy moments are treasured for a long time. For me it was those times when mom "peeked out" and I got a glimpse of her. Whether it was in the tilt of her head or in something she said, it brought a smile to my lips and joy to my heart.

When dealing with a heart wrenching issue such as this, a loved one suffering with dementia, it is very important to not fall back into our old way of problem and stress management. As I continued to travel the bumpy unknown road of dementia, my best friend was my support. She listened to me every day, as I cried on her shoulder. I do not know what I would have done if God had not given me my friend. And as unlikely as it seems, she was going through the same issue with her parents. What a wonderful God we have. We both could relate to each other because we were going through the same things at the same time. We have been friends since High School, through the good, the bad, and the ugly! Her support allowed joy to come in and laughter to come out. Having someone, like my friend, that you can talk to honestly is very important. There were days I had hardly pulled out of my mom's drive way and I was saying, "Google call my friend". It is important to really talk to your friends, get it all out, because you need to talk about today. Tomorrow is another day.

Another thing to keep you going on your bumpy, unknown, road is to remember what the Lord has done for you. My mom lived 45 minutes away from my home. As I drove to see her I would have my Kindle read Scripture out loud to me. I wanted to arrive prayed up and powered up. After the Scripture time, I would spend time in prayer, (eyes open of course!) then I Praised God for the things He had done for me in the past. I sang for joy because the Lord had directed my husband and me to a wonderful Bible believing Church full of Christians, many whom have become my friends. As I arrive at mom's home, I am full of joy, praising the Lord, prayed up and powered up. Ready for the day.

Many days it was a very good thing I arrived ready for the day, because as mom's dementia progressed, some days it was difficult to stay in harmony with her. I remember the day she forgot who I was. We were at her home and she looked at me after I had helped her with a task, and she said, "I do not know who you are, but you are really smart". Her statement took my breath away. Of course she had no awareness of the impact her statement had on me. She was onto the next thing that was fleeting through her mind. Now, myself, I was frozen to the floor. This was the first day she did not remember me. After that it happened on a regular occasion. The interesting thing was that mom never forgot my husband's name. After my dad died my husband became her go to guy. If she needed something done my husband would do it for her. She often said over the years that my husband rescued her. During the time that she dealt with dementia she never forgot who my husband was. Now myself, she remembered how smart I was, but did not have a clue who I was!

That first day mom forgot who I was, that was a real kick in the stomach. I knew that day would arrive, but did not anticipate it would be today. Wrong. Today was The Day. I got in my car to return home and the first thing I did was say, "Google, call my daughter." I knew that after a day like that I needed a joy infusion that evening. There was nothing better for a joy infusion for me than a visit from my daughter, son-in-law and my grandchildren. They are such a joy blessing to me, and so needed after the day I had experienced. I thank God for joy blessings, blessings just waiting to bless your socks off and ring your joy meter.

As I continued my drive home God was right there beside me. I felt His arms surrounding me like never before. One of my favorite scriptures is:

> And the Holy Spirit helps us in our weakness, for example, we don't know what God wants us to pray for. But the Holy Spirit prays for us with groaning's that cannot be expressed in words. (Romans 8:26)

I prayed this scripture. I was so emotional I did not know what to say or how to pray. So I gave it all to the Holy Spirit. Confident that between God and the Holy Spirit mom and I were well taken care of.

Good friends are an important part of maintaining a joyful life. Good friends help us, as they give us someone to talk to and someone to bounce ideas off of. The good friends are also important for keeping the joy stealers away from us because they help us keep the armor of God on. Just as good friends are important for the loved ones/care givers good friends are also important for the person going through the dementia process. It is very difficult to maintain any kind of, "normal" routine. Many people do not want to be around your loved one. Dementia is difficult in a social setting. The joy stealers love to sit there and rob as much joy as they can. It is important to kick those joy stealers out! Friends are a blessing. And we rejoice and thank God for blessings! Remembering this and acknowledging it will send those joy stealers right out the door!

Mom was blessed with loyal friends. Several that had been friends for years and years. One of her friends and her had been friends since high school. Now that was a long time! Her kids and my brother and I were friends before we were born. Early in moms dementia I went with her to visit this friend in Arizona. What a wonderful visit mom had! Friends like that help you get through the bad times. Another one of mom's friends was committed to meeting every Wednesday when possible. Every Wednesday. Sometimes I went with mom if I was free, but mom and her friend met every week. As mom's dementia progressed I took her to lunch with this friend of ours. Her daughter-in-law came a long, so it was lunch for the four of us. Mom and this lovely woman had been friends since I was very young. As you can imagine in the beginning of the dementia journey our lunches were very normal; conversation, love and laughter. As the dementia journey continued I began having to order lunch for mom, just a slight bump on this unknown road in our journey, but we managed and it did not lessen our joy. Often mom talked of the four of us going off on vacation together. Mom and her friend had taken many vacations together. Often those conversations turned to laughter as we recalled memories of those vacations and helped mom 'remember' them. As the dementia journey was progressing we continued meeting. Sometimes, perhaps often, the lunch was difficult, but always there was joy and laughter, and after? Tears came, tears of sadness and yes, tears of joy, for when you love, part of the tears are for grieving, and part of the tears are for joy and thanksgiving, for the beautiful friend you have had.

I have always thanked God for giving my family such wonderful friends. These families have been a part of my life almost as long as I can remember. I thank God that they were such wonderful, faithful friends to mom. It is to my ultimate joy that we are still meeting for our Wednesday lunches. Where the joy stealers tried to come in, they were met by friendship and love and laughter. Take that joy stealers! Love and joy and laughter, smoothed the bumps in the road ahead.

Friends are really one solid way to keep joy in our hearts. After my dad died mom met a man who had many of the same interests that she did. They slowly fell in love and he became a part of our family. During mom's journey with dementia, he was there at every step. Ever so slowly he began to have to be involved more and more in mom's every day care. He very lovingly did everything necessary to take care of mom. The road became very difficult on him as it was mainly all on his shoulders. As much as I tried to take some of the load, mom relied on him for everything.

As the dementia progressed mom fell one day and was taken to the emergency room. Well, at that point things went downhill fast. She did not understand where she was, or why she was there. She did not know who these people were and why they were, "doing things", to her. As she was admitted to the hospital we tried to calm her down but we were not successful. She became very combative and kept saying she wanted to go "home". Now she had been seeking God in her own way, for some time. I had been trying to set up a time to bring her to Church with me, but had yet to make that work. As we left the hospital that night none of us had a good feeling. The joy stealers were there and had taken our joy.

When morning came, so I could call the hospital and see how she was, I found out she was doing very well. I was like "What?" The nursing supervisor came on the phone and said I hope you do not mind, but your mom was seeking God last night so a couple of nurses took her to the Chapel and she had a "God Experience", meeting God and now she is calm and joyful. I was speechless! Then I was filled to joy unending. I said, "Mind, I am so thankful." We got up to the hospital to see her and she not only was calm and smiling, she was glowing!

> When Moses came down Mount Sinai carrying the two
> stone tablets inscribed with the terms of the Covenant,
> he wasn't aware that his face had become radiant because
> he had spoken to the Lord. (Exodus 34:29)

Mom had a "God Experience", and her face was radiant. She was no longer confused, she was joyful and calm. God can communicate with anyone, no matter their mental or emotional state. As hospital staff entered her room they could not believe she was the same person as the day before. Meeting God will do that for you. But for my husband and I, one of the most amazing things was mom would stop right in the middle of a conversation, (well, as much conversation as she could do), she would stop and say, "Wait, do you hear them, do you hear the angels singing?" Then, she would tilt her head like she was listening. She did that all day and even the next day. She listened to the angels singing, and I can tell you from the look on her face the singing sounded beautiful.

It was decided by all the powers that be, that what would be best for mom was to move into a nursing home. My brother and his wife had driven the 8 hours to be with mom and her friend and my husband and I during this difficult time. This difficult time was made so much easier by a wonderful group of nurses who took mom to meet Jesus. Every time mom asked, "do you hear the angels?" joy soared in our hearts. After talking with mom's friend, he was kind and said I had been driving the 45 minutes to see her. It was time for him to do the driving. So she went into a nursing home in the town I live in, just a few minutes from my home.

After all the paperwork was done we drove mom to the nursing home. With the help of my brother and his wife we got mom admitted and settled in the nursing home. This began a long journey of nursing home visits. I entered the nursing home each day with a smile and joy to share. My goal was to talk to who I could and share joy and Jesus all around. Mom loved the nursing home. Of course, not every minute of every day, but for the most part. It warmed my heart that every time I visited she asked if it was time for Church. The nursing home had Church Services on Sunday afternoons. Mom loved attending these services. She had a difficult time remembering almost everything, yet at the Sunday Services when we started singing she remembered the words to all the old hymns. Oh, how I loved to sit next to her and listen to her sing the hymns! Maybe she was singing along with the angels.

There was a woman there in the Alzheimer's Unit with mom who had lost her ability to speak. That happens in the progression of the disease. This woman made noises and I believe she thought she was speaking and making words. But, the more discouraged she got, the louder she got, and the more everyone avoided her. I felt very bad for her. So one day. I went up to her wheel chair and knelt down and patted her hair and looked right in her eyes and said very quietly that I was sorry that I did not understand her, but that she was very beautiful today and that I loved her and so did Jesus. She smiled so big. And right away calmed down. I believe God can communicate to us no matter what our mental condition. Just because we believe someone is beyond understanding does not limit what God can do.

> Jesus looked at them intently and said, humanly speaking, it is impossible, but not with God. Everything is possible with God. (Mark 10:27)

There came a time that mom developed pneumonia and was transferred to the hospital. The pneumonia became difficult to treat, perhaps because of a lifetime of asthma and diabetes. She began to struggle again. My husband and my daughter and I sat by her bedside or stood and held her hand to calm her. The most awesome thing I have ever experienced was my daughter hugging her grandmother and singing, "Jesus loves me" - written by William B. Bradbury, to her. It was extra beautiful as I had an echo of mom singing that very song at the previous Sunday Church Service.

YES, JESUS LOVES ME, YES, JESUS LOVES ME, YES JESUS LOVES ME,

THE BIBLE TELLS ME SO.

As the last sound faded away, in my mind it was the sound of both of them singing together, it sounded like angels singing. I looked over and mom was sleeping calmly. My daughter and I had tears trailing down our faces. Sadness yet joy, because we knew my mom was resting in Jesus's arms.

Love and Joy Unending

THE END

AUTHORS NOTE

Dear readers, thank you for spending your time in the study of joy. It is my prayer that somewhere between the covers you read something that made you smile. May God direct your path and lead you to your joy.

Joyfully yours,
Joni

Printed in the United States
By Bookmasters